—— BEEKMAN 1802 ——

A SEAT AT THE TABLE

BEEKMAN 1802

A SEAT AT THE TABLE

Recipes to Nourish Your
Family, Friends, and Community

BRENT RIDGE & JOSH KILMER-PURCELL
WITH OUR NEIGHBOR,
ROSE MARIE TRAPANI

PHOTOGRAPHY BY
CHRISTIAN WATSON

For information about permission to reproduce selections from this book, write to trade.
permissions@hmhco.com or to Permissions, Houghton Mifflin Harcourt Publishing Company,
3 Park Avenue, 19th Floor, New York, New York 10016.

www.hmhco.com

Library of Congress Cataloging-in-Publication Data is available.

Names: Ridge, Brent, author. | Kilmer-Purcell, Josh, date, author. | Trapani,
Rose M., author.
Title: Beekman 1802, a seat at the table : recipes to nourish your family,
friends, and community / Brent Ridge, Josh Kilmer-Purcell, and Rose Marie
Trapani.
Description: Boston : Houghton Mifflin Harcourt, 2017. | Includes index.
Identifiers: LCCN 2017019016 (print) | LCCN 2017018461 (ebook) | ISBN
9780544850224 (ebook) | ISBN 9780544850217 (paper over board) | ISBN
9780544850224 (ebk)
Subjects: LCSH: Cooking, American. | Seasonal cooking. | Farm produce—New
York (State)—Upstate New York. | Beekman 1802 Farm (N.Y.) | LCGFT:
Cookbooks.
Classification: LCC TX715 (print) | LCC TX715 .R7238 2017 (ebook) | DDC
641.5973—dc23
LC record available at https://lccn.loc.gov/2017019016

Book design by Alissa Faden

Printed in China
SCP 10 9 8 7 6 5 4 3 2 1

To all of those neighbors around the world who invited us to have a seat when we had nothing but our gratitude to bring to the table.

CONTENTS

INTRODUCTION 9

FALL 13 · SPRING 133

WINTER 81 · SUMMER 191

ACKNOWLEDGMENTS 247

ABOUT THE AUTHORS 248

INDEX 250

Introduction

This is a love story.

From the moment that we stepped foot at Beekman we knew that the farm would grow to be bigger than its fences. As the farm grew, it not only reimagined our own lives but also revitalized the entire village of Sharon Springs, New York. Something else happened, too. As the boundaries of Beekman grew to other cities, other states, and even other countries, so did the number of Beekman "neighbors." From all walks of life, all ethnicities and orientations, we formed an ad hoc community of believers. Not just devotees of farm to table, but the visionnaires of our own movement, *farm AS table.*

Our farm sits in an odd vortex. The entire area was called Beekman's Corners at one point in time. On one side of the farm stretches the rest of Schoharie County—a swath of the Mohawk Valley with some of the richest glacial agricultural soil in the world. It's known as the "breadbasket of the American Revolution" because so much of the food that went to feed the hungry army originated here. On the western border is the village of Sharon Springs, once one of the most famous spa towns in the world. In the early 1900s thousands of people crowded the streets as they rushed to bathe in the miracle mineral waters that sprang forth from the earth.

In the bustling summer months, the farm families would often travel into the village and watch the comings and goings of the hoi polloi such as the Rockefellers and the Vanderbilts and even Oscar Wilde. It was social climbing as spectator sport.

For generations, these two worlds intertwined, and as summer-long spa vacations became less fashionable and as America's agricultural production moved to areas with longer growing seasons, the inhabitants on both sides of the Beekman held hands as they walked steadily down into nearly a century of economic decline.

Since founding Beekman 1802 in 2008 and bringing together a collective of rural artisans and food-makers under one umbrella, the community has once again clasped hands, working together not just to rebuild but to rebirth, reinvigorate, reengage, and reinvent. Collectively we've rediscovered the power of community (and apparently hand-holding), and people from around the world now travel to our mecca for one reason—because around every corner and every bend in the road what you see for miles and miles is nothing but potential.

When we open the barn doors or the village rolls out the welcome mat for visitors it's with a sense of pride.

Everyone has a seat at the table.

And it is still true, no matter how old you are—when you go out into
the world it is best to hold hands and stick together.

ROBERT FULGHUM

PART ONE

FALL

Ricotta-Filled Figs Wrapped in Prosciutto

MAKES 12 APPETIZERS

These morsels looks almost too pretty eat, but ultimately everyone will give into their sweet and salty temptation.

>>>>> ⚡ *Shared at the table with…* ⚡ <<<<<

_____

_____

_____

_____

[Some people] have a wonderful capacity to appreciate again and again, freshly and naively, the basic goods of life, with awe, pleasure, wonder, and even ecstasy.

—A. H. Maslow

12 fresh figs

1 cup ricotta

¼ cup confectioners' sugar

1 tablespoon mini chocolate chips

⅛ teaspoon finely grated lemon zest

⅛ teaspoon pure vanilla extract

6 thin slices prosciutto, halved lengthwise

Honey for serving

Wash figs and blot dry. Cut stems off the figs and cut a cross on the top of each, halfway through the fig, to make an opening about ½ inch wide. In a small bowl, mix the ricotta, sugar, chocolate chips, zest, and vanilla. Fill the figs and wrap each fig with half a slice of prosciutto, folding down the edges to look like a flower petal.

Arrange on a plate and drizzle with honey.

USING GRAPE LEAVES

- Season a boneless chicken breast with salt and pepper, then wrap it in the grape leaves. Secure them with a strip of bacon wrapped around the outside of the leaves. Bake at 350°F for about 20 minutes, or until juices run clear when pierced.

- Make stuffed grape leaves. For each one, place two tablespoons leftover rice or risotto in the center of a leaf and roll up, tucking in the sides. Drizzle with olive oil and balsamic vinegar. Serve stuffed leaves with a salad or as an appetizer.

- Use as garnish on a cheese plate.

- Shred leaves and use them as a relish on sandwiches.

Brined Grape Leaves

MAKES 1 QUART (30 LEAVES)

About 30 fresh grape leaves

2 slices of lemon

1 tablespoon pickling salt

2 tablespoons white vinegar

Wash the leaves and remove their stems by snipping a small triangle out of the bottom of the leaf. (You can use kitchen shears for this step.) Stack the leaves in stacks of 8 or 10. Carefully roll them up like cigars and place them into a clean quart-size canning jar, periodically adding a lemon slice. Repeat until the jar is full.

In a small pot, make a brine by bringing 2 cups of water and the pickling salt to the boil. Add the vinegar. Pour the brine into the jar, making sure that all of the rolls of leaves are completely covered. Tuck an extra grape leaf over the rolls to make sure they all stay below the brine. Allow jar to cool to room temperature and then store in the refrigerator for up to 3 months.

Rinse leaves before using.

Wild grapes grow throughout upstate New York where the Beekman Mansion is located, but you can use the leaf of any cultivated vine as long as you pick the leaves when they are young and tender (and before any bugs take a bite). Keep a few quarts of these leaves in the refrigerator to use for making stuffed grape leaves or as a decorative element on an antipasto platter of Italian cured meats and cheeses.

>>>>> *Shared at the table with...* <<<<<

_____

_____

_____

_____

Beekman Burnt Broccoli Soup

MAKES 6 SERVINGS

Josh cannot be trusted with the broiler. He's been known to set two different timers and STILL let something burn. We often drizzle broccoli with a little olive oil and shaved garlic and put it under the broiler to give just a bit of a char. Josh can't go wrong! When prepared this way, this traditional broccoli soup recipe takes on an unexpected smokiness and depth.

>>>>> *Shared at the table with...* <<<<<

1½ pounds broccoli, cut into florets

8 garlic cloves, thinly sliced

1 onion, halved and sliced

3 tablespoons olive oil

1 tablespoon fresh lemon juice

1 teaspoon kosher salt

1 bay leaf

1 large potato, peeled and diced

4 cups vegetable broth

⅛ teaspoon white pepper

1 cup milk

½ cup grated Parmigiano cheese

Extra-virgin olive oil for garnish (optional)

Preheat oven to 425°F.

In a large bowl, toss broccoli with garlic, onion, oil, and juice to coat. Line a baking sheet with foil and brush with more oil. Spread vegetables on the baking sheet in a single layer. Sprinkle with salt. Roast until broccoli has browned—about 20 minutes. Reserve a few florets for garnish.

Place roasted vegetables in a large saucepan and add bay leaf, potato, broth, and white pepper. Bring to a boil over medium-high heat. Reduce heat to medium, cover, and simmer 15 minutes. Remove bay leaf. Add milk and simmer for 5 more minutes. Add half the grated cheese, and stir to blend. Taste and add more salt if necessary.

Use an immersion blender to purée the soup. You may also purée the soup in a blender or food processor, working in batches depending on the size of your appliance.

Ladle the puréed soup into bowls and garnish with remaining cheese, reserved roasted broccoli, and, if you like, a drizzle of extra-virgin olive oil.

Megan's Toasted Flour Soup

MAKES 4 SERVINGS

12 cloves, whole

1 medium onion, peeled and halved horizontally

7 tablespoons butter

6 tablespoons flour

1 bay leaf

Salt

Heat 8 cups of water to the boiling point and then keep at simmer.

Insert 6 whole cloves into each onion half.

In a medium-heavy saucepan, melt 6 tablespoons of the butter over medium heat. Add the flour and cook, stirring constantly with a wooden spoon, until the mixture is smooth and the color of chocolate—7 to 10 minutes. Do not let the mixture scorch. (If it does, throw it out and start over.)

Remove the butter and flour from heat. Gradually add the hot water by ladleful, stirring constantly until the mixture is smooth. Add the clove-spiked onion halves, bay leaf, and salt to taste. Simmer over the lowest possible heat, stirring occasionally, for 1 hour.

Remove onion and bay leaf before serving. Swirl in the last tablespoon of butter.

Note: You may garnish this soup with roasted vegetables.

When Megan told us about a soup recipe of her mom's that is largely comprised of flour, we were very skeptical. However, she had also introduced us to "shugy butter bread"—slices of white bread coated with butter and dipped in sugar—which is delicious, as is this soup. Serving the soup to guests also makes for an interesting conversation starter at cold-weather dinner table gatherings.

>>>> Shared at the <<<<
table with…

_____

_____

_____

_____

_____

No-Knead Italian Bread

MAKES A 1½-POUND LOAF

Once you make Italian bread using this recipe, there's no way you'll want to eat Italian bread made any other way. The reason it's called no-knead is because the bread is not kneaded, but does have a long rising time of 12 to 18 hours to create a risen texture. For best results, this bread should be baked in a covered clay pan or a covered cast-iron or ceramic pot. The inspiration for this recipe was an article published in the New York Times several years ago that featured a revolutionary no-knead bread by Jim Lahey of Sullivan Street Bakery. In addition to making bread, you can use this recipe to make dough for pizza and focaccia.

>>>> *Shared at the table with…* <<<<

1 cup semolina flour

1 cup 00 flour (cake flour may be substituted)

1 cup all-purpose flour

1½ teaspoons salt

¼ teaspoon instant yeast

Extra semolina flour for dusting and coating

Combine semolina flour, 00 flour, all-purpose flour, salt, and yeast in a large bowl. Add 1¼ lukewarm water and stir the mixture until the ingredients are blended. Cover the bowl with a sheet of plastic wrap to keep in the moisture, and let the dough rise at least 12 hours at room temperature (between 65° and 75°F). After this time, the surface of the dough should be covered with small bubbles and the dough should have risen significantly.

Run a spoon around the bowl to deflate the dough. Use the spoon to fold the dough over itself. Let the dough rest 15 minutes. Meanwhile, spread about ¼ cup of semolina flour onto a cotton dish towel. Take dough out of the bowl and use your hands to shape the dough into a rectangle or ball, depending on the shape of your baking pan. Fold the dough into thirds and place the dough seam-side down on the dishtowel. Sprinkle some more semolina on the bread. Bring the sides of the towel over the bread to cover. Let rise 2 hours. By this time the dough should be about double its original size.

Meanwhile, when the dough has risen about 1½ hours, place an oven rack in the middle position and preheat the oven to 450°F. Place a clay-covered pot, a heavy covered cast-iron pot, or a ceramic pot in the oven. Heat the pot in the oven for 30 minutes.

Continued

BRAIDING ITALIAN BREAD

To braid the bread as shown, after the initial rise, flour a board or surface with ¼ cup of all-purpose flour and turn the dough out onto it. Deflate the dough by pressing and kneading the flour into the dough until the dough no longer feels sticky. Roll it into a long loaf. Cut the loaf into 3 equal pieces and, using your hands, roll each piece evenly into a rope about 12 inches long. Place the ropes on a parchment-lined baking sheet. Braid the bread starting in the middle of the ropes. Take the left rope and cross it over the middle piece. Take the right rope and cross it over the rope that is now in the middle. Repeat crossing left over center, followed by right over center until you reach the end, as if you're braiding hair. Pinch the bottom ends together and tuck them under the loaf. Repeat for the other side. Cover and let rise until doubled in size, then bake as directed.

No-Knead Italian Bread

Remove the pot from the oven and place the dough into the pot seam side up. Cover the pot and bake 30 minutes. Uncover and bake until the bread is brown on the outside—an additional 10 minutes or so.

Remove the loaf from the pot and cool on a wire rack.

Note: To simplify the recipe, you can substitute King Arthur brand bread flour in place of the semolina, 00, or all-purpose flour.

Garlic Knots

8 tablespoons butter, softened

8 garlic cloves, minced

1 tablespoon chopped fresh parsley (you can substitute your favorite herb)

Flour, for dusting

1 pound Breakfast of Champions Pizza Dough (page 208) or store-bought pizza dough, room temperature

¼ cup shredded mozzarella

2 tablespoons Parmigiano cheese

Freshly cracked pepper

The rich, volcanic soils of our county are perfect for growing garlic, and one stop at the annual garlic festival will show you the hundreds of ways the locals have found to put garlic to good use. Easy and crowd-pleasing, these buttery, cheesy bites are perfect for game day or any other day.

Shared at the table with…

Move an oven rack to the middle position and preheat the oven to 375°F. Line a baking sheet with parchment.

In a small bowl, combine the butter, garlic, and parsley. On a lightly floured surface, stretch the pizza dough into a 12-inch by 8-inch rectangle. Spread butter mixture over dough. Sprinkle with mozzarella, Parmigiano, and pepper to taste.

Fold the dough in half lengthwise and press edges together to seal, then flatten dough with your hands to form a long rectangle. Cut into 24 strips, 4 inches long by ½ inch wide.

Stretch each strip and tie into a knot. Place the knots onto the prepared baking sheet. Bake 20 minutes or until golden brown.

These can be served warm or at room temperature.

Pesto Trapanese

MAKES 6 TO 8 SERVINGS

Just like the village of Sharon Springs and just like this cookbook, great things can happen when neighbors work together. Pesto Trapanese is a very old recipe dating back to ancient times when Genovese mariners from Northern Italy stopped at the port of Trapani, Sicily. They brought their recipe for garlic-walnut pesto, to which Trapanese sailors added local ingredients—such as tomato, almonds, parsley, and mint—and Pesto Trapanese was born.

Pesto Trapanese is traditionally made by hand in a mortar and pestle and served as a first course with a strand pasta such as bucatini or spaghetti; this course is followed by fish, fried eggplant, roasted potatoes, or fried sausages. Sometimes the pasta is topped with fresh breadcrumbs to add texture, or with fried eggplant as another variety of the pasta course. We include both the traditional preparation method and the modern food processor version for this recipe.

>>>→ *Shared at the table with…* ←←←←

1½ pounds ripe plum tomatoes

4 ounces blanched almonds

4 garlic cloves, peeled

¾ cup fresh basil leaves plus 25 leaves for garnish

¾ cup fresh parsley

12 mint leaves

1 teaspoon sea salt

½ teaspoon black pepper

¼ teaspoon red pepper flakes or crushed pepperoncino

¾ cup extra-virgin olive oil

1 pound bucatini or spaghetti

½ cup Pecorino Romano

PESTO, PREPARED BY HAND

In a large pot of boiling water, cook the tomatoes 10 seconds to blanch and then run under cold water. Peel, halve, seed, and chop the tomatoes. Place in large bowl and set aside.

Place almonds and garlic into a mortar and grind with pestle until creamy. Add the ¾ cup basil, the parsley, and mint; grind until the herbs are incorporated. Transfer the mixture to the bowl with the tomatoes. Season with salt, pepper, and red pepper flakes. Add the oil and gently mix together with a wooden spoon. Cover the bowl with plastic wrap and refrigerate until needed.

PESTO, PREPARED WITH A FOOD PROCESSOR

In a large pot of boiling water, cook the tomatoes 10 seconds to blanch and then run under cold water. Peel, halve, seed, and chop the tomatoes. Place in bowl and set aside.

Continued

Pasta con Pesto alla Trapanese

6 large ripe plum tomatoes - 1½ lbs.
  Blanched - Remove seeds - small
4 oz. Blanched Almonds -
4 medium sized garlic cloves - peeled
¾ cup basil leaves ± (25 large leaves) ground
¾ cup parsley leaves - 10 sprigs
12 mint leaves - chopped
1 tsp. Kosher salt (sea)
12 twists of black pepper
¼ tsp. red pepper flakes
¾ cup olive oil
½ c. pecorino

1 lb. pasta or Spaghetti
  cook reserve 1 cup
of
          for garnish :

      large bowl & set aside.
      mash the almonds
      mixture is creamy :
      grind until the
      porated. To serve
      bowl or crock
      smallest dice
      bowl containing
      son with salt
      to taste, add
      ly with a wood
      refrigerate until

Pesto Trapanese

In a food processor, purée the almonds, garlic, and oil until creamy. Add the ¾ cup basil, the parsley, mint, salt, black pepper, and red pepper flakes; pulse until creamy.

Transfer mixture to a large crockery or glass bowl, add the tomatoes, and mix until blended.

FOR PASTA

In a large pot of boiling salted water, cook the pasta until al dente. Drain, reserving 1 cup of cooking water.

While the pasta is cooking, line a serving platter with the 25 basil leaves.

Gradually add enough of the reserved pasta cooking water to the pesto sauce to thin the sauce to the desired consistency. Remove half of the sauce and set aside. Add the drained pasta to the bowl with the remaining sauce, tossing to coat. Pour the coated pasta onto the serving platter lined with basil leaves, and spoon the remaining pesto sauce over the pasta. Sprinkle the grated Pecorino cheese over the pasta and serve.

ARTISAN PROFILE

ROSE MARIE TRAPANI

HERE IS HOW THE BEEKMAN 1802 farm table got started . . . around a pot of boiling water.

Sharing food after a day of hard work is nothing new to our part of the country. Big celebratory meals often followed the harvest of the hops crop (the origin of "let's go to the hop"). The Amish communities surrounding us can raise a barn in a day and then feast into the night. Even the ladies at a quilting bee know how to sup after the pattern has formed and the last knot tied.

When we settled at Beekman Farm, we knew nothing about farming, and we literally started building our community by knocking on the doors of our neighbors. Paul at the next farm over taught us how to raise pigs in the foundation of our old barn silo. Church lady Cookson and her husband Peter taught us how to humanely crack the neck of our first chicken. Barb just on the other side of Slate Hill introduced us to a hundred new varieties of heirloom vegetables, and without George, the 32 bee hives in our apiary surely wouldn't be as happy.

As one might imagine, "breaking in" as new farmers requires a lot of breaking bread, and one table that we found ourselves at more than any other belonged to our neighbor Rose Marie Trapani.

Having grown up in Sicily, learning to cook from the women of her extended Italian family, there's a joy and effortlessness to her meal preparation that seems to be lost in the modern hustle and bustle that most of us face.

At one meal, as Rose Marie presented plate after plate of delicious food, she recounted a typical day in her childhood home. Her father worked in the fields. At precisely noon, the men of the village would leave their posts and filter their way down the small streets to their homes where they had exactly 22 minutes to eat their lunch before heading back to punch in on the time clock.

Continued

Rose Marie's mom had the daily routine down to a science. Twelve minutes before Rose Marie's father would arrive, the pot of water was put onto the stove to boil. She would then start cutting up whatever fresh vegetable she had on hand. Six minutes prior to the door opening, the pasta went into the pot of boiling water followed two minutes later by the vegetables. By the time the hand was on the door knob and the work boots on the threshold, the plate of food was on the kitchen table and cheese was being grated on top.

And how does Rose Marie pass along this culinary history? By feeding the neighborhood. There's hardly a house in a 20-mile radius that hasn't harbored a piece of her Tupperware. Many a time we've come home late at night from travel to find our refrigerator completely full of delights.

As Beekman 1802 grows bigger and bigger and our lives increasingly busier, we still manage to sit down to dinner every night. We make time to do it even if all the time we have is 22 minutes.

Homemade Tomato Paste

MAKES ABOUT 1½ POUNDS PASTE

Historically, tomato paste did not come from a tin can! In Italy, all of the neighbors would help each other during the tomato harvest to create pots of this paste, which could be used to make tomato sauce when the tomato pickings were slimmer. The tomato purée was spread on big slabs of wood set up on sawhorses to dry in the sun. Young children helped by turning the tomato purée from time to time. This communal pantry-stocking was a lot of fun. The resulting estratto *(tomato paste) was spooned into earthen jars, covered with olive oil, and set in a cool pantry to use during the winter months.*

If you live in an area (like Sharon Springs!) where the weather isn't ideal for drying tomato purée in the sun, you can still make your own tomato paste by using the oven. This is an all-day project, but well worth the culinary experience and a welcome boost of fresh tomato flavor that you just can't get from a can.

⟫⟫⟫→ *Shared at the table with…* ←⟪⟪⟪

_____

_____

_____

_____

10 pounds ripe Roma plum tomatoes, cut into quarters

¼ cup olive oil, plus more for greasing and sealing

3 garlic cloves, peeled and smashed

2 bay leaves

1 tablespoon kosher salt

½ teaspoon citric acid (you can substitute 2 tablespoons fresh lemon juice)

In a large saucepan, combine the tomatoes, oil, garlic, bay leaves, and salt and cook over medium heat until the tomatoes have softened and their skins start to pull away—15 minutes. Discard bay leaves. Stir in citric acid.

Place a food mill over another large saucepan. Push the tomatoes through the food mill, leaving the skins and seeds behind. Discard skins and seeds. Cook the tomatoes over medium heat, stirring occasionally, until very thick. This may take up to 2 hours.

Meanwhile, move two oven racks to the middle positions, and preheat the oven to 300°F. Rub two rimmed baking sheets (18- by 13-inch sheets are ideal) lightly with olive oil and set aside.

When the tomato puree is very thick, spread it onto the baking sheets. The purée should be about ½ inch thick on the sheets. Bake the purée in the oven, using a spatula to stir it every 20 minutes. Continue to bake, periodically switching the position of the baking sheets so that the purée reduces evenly. As the purée reduces, it will shrink on the baking sheets. Combine the purée onto one baking sheet when it shrinks enough to fit in one layer. Keep an eye on it; you don't want it to burn. The paste is finished when it has a very thick texture and a deep brick-red color. This will take from 3 to 4 hours.

Note

To use, cool paste and divide into ½-pint jars, leaving ¾ inch of headspace. Top jars with a layer of olive oil and store in the refrigerator. Use paste to make a quick tomato sauce or as a spread on crostini.

Lemon Garlic Sauce

MAKES ABOUT ½ CUP SAUCE

4 garlic cloves

1 teaspoon kosher salt

½ cup extra virgin
olive oil

Juice of 1 large lemon

2 teaspoons dried
oregano

2 tablespoons chopped
fresh parsley

Crush garlic with the salt in a mortar and pestle until creamy. Add olive oil, lemon juice, oregano (crush the oregano with your hands to release the oils), and parsley. Stir well.

Note: This sauce will keep in the refrigerator in a closed glass jar for up to three days, but you will need to let it come to room temperature before using, as the olive oil will congeal.

Lemon garlic sauce is wonderful on grilled chicken, fish, and vegetables.

To infuse extra flavor when using this sauce while grilling meat, make an oregano brush. Start with five oregano sprigs, 5 to 7 inches in length. Strip about 3 inches of leaves off the bottom of each stalk, and tie the stripped ends of the stalks together to make a brush. Use this instead of a pastry brush to brush the sauce onto whatever you're grilling.

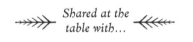
Shared at the table with…

Beet Greens Sautéed with Garlic and Breadcrumbs

MAKES 4 SERVINGS

The farm seems to have the perfect growing conditions for beets. We've not had a growing season yet when we didn't have more than enough. Because of the abundance of beet greens (the leafy tops of the beet root), we like to take this recipe to potluck dinners. We can make lots of it, its earthy-yet-mild flavors pair with almost anything others are likely to bring, and a lot of people have never prepared the greens before. It's an opportunity to share something new!

⇉⇉⇉ *Shared at the table with…* ⇇⇇⇇

_____

_____

_____

_____

GARNISH

1 large tomato, diced

1 tablespoon olive oil

¼ teaspoon minced garlic

1 tablespoon chopped fresh basil

GREENS

2 tablespoons olive oil

3 garlic cloves, thinly sliced

¼ teaspoon red pepper flakes

1 pound beet greens, washed and drained

Salt and pepper

½ cup panko bread crumbs

1 tablespoon grated Pecorino Romano cheese

Start by making the garnish. In a small bowl stir together the tomato, oil, garlic, and basil. Set aside.

To make the greens, in a large skillet, heat the oil over medium heat. Add the garlic and cook until golden—1 to 2 minutes. Add the pepper flakes and stir for a few seconds. Add greens and salt and pepper to taste, then cover and cook, stirring occasionally until wilted—5 minutes. Add the breadcrumbs and stir well to combine. Cook another 3 minutes to toast the breadcrumbs a bit. Transfer to a platter and garnish with the tomato mixture.

Sprinkle cheese over the dish just before serving.

While the spirit of neighborliness was important on the frontier
because neighbors were so few, it is even more important now
because our neighbors are so many.

LADY BIRD JOHNSON

Broccoli with Garlic

MAKES 4 SERVINGS

1 large head of broccoli, florets and stems separated

3 tablespoons olive oil

4 garlic cloves, thinly sliced

¼ teaspoon red pepper flakes

Salt and pepper

½ lemon

One of the simplest and simply perfect side dishes we make on the farm—even delicious when tossed into pasta or rice.

Shared at the table with…

With a sharp knife, peel the stem of broccoli and cut into spears. In a large pot of boiling salted water, cook the prepared stems with the florets until crisp-tender—3 to 5 minutes. Drain and run cold water over them to stop the cooking. Drain well and set aside.

In a large skillet, heat oil over medium heat. Add garlic and cook, stirring occasionally, until golden. Add pepper flakes and stir. Add the broccoli, turning to coat, and sauté a few minutes.

Season with salt and pepper to taste. Plate the broccoli and squeeze a little lemon juice over it before serving.

Homemade Pasta

3 cups all-purpose flour

4 large eggs

¾ teaspoon salt

2 teaspoons olive oil

Flour for rolling out pasta

Pasta is surprisingly easy to make when using a food processor, and a beautiful experience when making by hand. Invite some neighbors over and make an afternoon of it!

>>>> *Shared at the table with…* <<<<

_____

_____

_____

_____

TO MAKE USING A FOOD PROCESSOR

Place 2½ cups of the flour in the bowl of a food processor. In a measuring cup with a spout, lightly beat the eggs with the salt and oil. With the processor running, gradually pour the egg mixture through the feed tube into the flour mixture.

Add the remaining flour a little at a time and stop and pulse the processor until the dough forms a ball.

TO MAKE BY HAND

Place flour on a pastry board or other smooth surface and make a well in the middle. Place the eggs, salt, and oil in the well, and beat lightly with a fork. Using a fork, stir until well combined, gradually drawing in the flour from the sides. Then use the heel of your hand to knead, turning the dough over and then turning it again. Knead until the dough is smooth and no longer sticky—5 to 10 minutes. Form the dough into a ball.

Once dough is ready, wrap in plastic wrap and let rest for 30 minutes. Cut the dough in half; cover one half with plastic wrap. Flour a pastry board and use a rolling pin to roll out half of the dough so that it's about ⅛ inch thick. Let the pasta dry for 10 minutes; turn it over and dry 10 more minutes on the other side; and then cut into desired shapes. Repeat with other half of dough.

Continued

Alternatively, use a pasta machine to roll out and cut the dough. If using a hand-cranked machine, sprinkle extra flour on the dough surface before rolling it through the machine. The pasta will stretch in the machine, so you'll want to us only a portion, such as one-sixth of the dough, in the machine.

Allow the pasta to dry on a cotton dish towel dusted with flour 10 to 15 minutes before cutting. The pasta should feel dry to the touch.

Note: You may also use 00 or doppio zero flour (Italian flour) in place of the all-purpose flour. This flour is traditionally used for making pasta and is made from coarsely ground durum wheat. Italian flour is mixed with water to make tough pasta dough that holds its shape during cooking and will not disintegrate into a starchy paste.

Squash Manicotti

MAKES 6 TO 8 SERVINGS

To make an awe-inspiring presentation of this recipe, we used a nonstick bread loaf pan and stacked the stuffed manicotti. Once baked, we turned the pan upside down, allowing the loaf to slide out. This presentation is as pleasing to the eye as it is to the palate.

The butternut squash "noodles" in this dish only require a portion of the squash neck. Save the rest in the refrigerator for other dishes such as muffins, as an addition to soup, or to roast.

>>>>>> *Shared at the table with...* <<<<<<

_____

_____

_____

_____

1 large (2 to 2½ pounds) butternut squash

Olive oil spray

FILLING

2 tablespoons butter

⅛ teaspoon nutmeg

½ teaspoon salt

¼ teaspoon white pepper

1 cup freshly grated Parmigiano cheese

1 egg yolk

1 cup finely crushed amaretti cookies or almond macaroons,

1 pound manicotti or paccheri (large tubular pasta)

BÉCHAMEL SAUCE

3 cups goat or cow's milk

4 tablespoons unsalted butter

1 teaspoon salt

¼ teaspoon white pepper

¼ teaspoon nutmeg

¼ cup all-purpose flour

1 cup shredded mozzarella

½ cup grated Beekman 1802 Blaak goat cheese (mozzarella can be substituted)

¼ cup grated Parmigiano cheese

Preheat oven to 350°F.

Pierce the skin of the squash and microwave for 1 minute to make it easier to cut. Cut the butternut squash at the base of the neck; you will use the bulb to make your filling and the neck to make the "noodles." Cut both the neck and bulb portions into halves vertically and remove any seeds.

Spray the squash bulb halves with olive oil spray and place on a large baking sheet, flesh side down. Roast 40 minutes, until flesh is fork-tender.

Continued

To simplify this recipe you may use pre-packaged peeled
cubed butternut squash that you roast and puree or frozen
butternut squash purée available at most supermarkets.
You can also forego the elaborate stacking process and
stuff larger manicotti with the squash mixture. If choosing
to do this, spoon a layer of sauce on the bottom of a
baking dish and place cooked and stuffed manicotti in a
single layer over the sauce. Spread béchamel-squash sauce
over the manicotti and sprinkle grated cheese over the
pasta, then bake until hot and bubbly.

Squash Manicotti

Meanwhile, prepare the squash "noodles" with the squash neck. Peel the neck and thinly slice it into wide, lasagna-like strips. A mandolin will make slicing the squash much easier, but you can also use a knife. Line two standard size baking pans with aluminum foil. Spray the pans with olive oil spray and lay the squash "noodles" in the pans. Spray the noodles and bake alongside the squash for the filling for the last 10 minutes, until the squash noodles are pliable.

Remove the squash bulb and noodles from the oven. Now make the fillingWhen the squash bulb is cool enough to handle, peel and dice. Weigh 1½ pounds (approximately 4 cups of squash) and transfer to a food processor. Add butter, nutmeg, salt, and white pepper. Pulse on and off until mixture is smooth, 15 to 20 seconds, scraping down sides of bowl as needed. Reserve ½ cup for the sauce and set aside.

Transfer the rest of the mixture to a bowl, and stir in cheese, egg yolk, and cookie crumbs. Let filling sit until no longer warm—15 to 25 minutes. Spoon filling into a resealable plastic bag. Refrigerate while you cook the pasta and make the béchamel sauce.

Next, cook the pasta. In a large pot of boiling salted water, cook the pasta until al dente—about 8 minutes. Drain.

Now make the béchamel sauce. In a small saucepan, heat the milk over low heat until warm. In a separate medium, heavy-bottomed saucepan, melt butter over low heat. Add salt, white pepper, and nutmeg. Add the flour, raise the heat to medium and cook, stirring constantly, until smooth, pale golden, and nutty. Gradually add the warmed milk, stirring constantly. Simmer the sauce until it is lightly thickened and coats the back of the spoon—about 5 minutes. Set aside.

Now you're ready to assemble the manicotti. Preheat the oven to 375°F.

Cut a corner off the bag with the squash filling and pipe filling into the pasta tubes. Grease a loaf pan, line with parchment paper, and spoon a thin layer of béchamel onto the bottom and arrange filled pasta tubes in a row one layer deep. Sprinkle with some of the mozzarella and Blaak cheeses, then add another thin layer of béchamel. Follow with another layer of filled pasta tubes. Repeat layering until you have filled the loaf pan. You should have some béchamel sauce remaining, which you will use to plate the manicotti.

Once you have filled the pan, top with a final layer of squash "noodles." Spray with olive oil spray. Cover with aluminum foil. Bake for 45 minutes. Let rest 15 minutes, then run a rubber spatula gently around the pan to loosen. Turn upside down onto a platter and gently remove paper. Cut into slices.

Add the ½ cup reserved squash purée to remaining béchamel sauce and mix well. Heat the sauce for plating. Ladle some sauce into each pasta bowl, place a slice of manicotti on it, and serve with grated Parmigiano cheese.

FARMER JOHN

SOMETIMES YOU FIND YOURSELF in the middle of nowhere, and sometimes in the middle of nowhere you find yourself.

We bought the Beekman Farm in 2007 thinking it was going to be a weekend getaway from our lives in the city. At the time, and with our youthful idealism, we thought the future looked bright. We cashed in everything we had ever saved and took out a million-dollar mortgage. (A million-dollar mortgage!)

One weekend we arrived at the farm to find a hand-written note in our mailbox.

> *My name is John Hall. I grew up in the area on a dairy farm, and I now have a herd of 80 goats. I am losing the place where I am farming. Could I please bring my goats to your property to graze? Otherwise I will have to sell them.*

A hand-written letter by a man down on his luck turned out to be our own salvation.

We both lost our jobs in the recession of 2008 and came very close to losing the farm, but we had our community and we had our bootstraps and that's the way Beekman 1802 started.

When life gives you lemons, you make lemonade. When life gives you goats, you make anything you can with the milk.

After nearly 10 years, Farmer John still lives on the property with us, now with 147 goats in the herd. The products inspired by the farm can be found around the world.

One neighbor helps another . . . and so on and so on and so on.

Club Roast Turkey

MARINADE

½ cup corn oil

1 teaspoon Bell's poultry seasoning or other chicken seasoning

2½ teaspoons kosher salt

1 tablespoon smoked paprika

¼ teaspoon black pepper

1 tablespoon minced garlic

TURKEY

One 12- to 14-pound turkey, giblets and neck removed and reserved

A few sprigs of fresh thyme

1 teaspoon kosher salt

1 small onion, peeled and halved

1 celery stalk, halved crosswise

A few sprigs of parsley

1 lemon, halved

8 strips bacon

YOGURT–SOUR CREAM HERB SAUCE

8 ounces yogurt

8 ounces sour cream

½ cup fresh dill

¼ cup fresh parsley

¼ cup basil leaves

1 garlic clove, chopped

2 tablespoons lemon juice

Salt and pepper

It was the Iroquois who came first, and ever since our remote little village nestled in the Mohawk Valley of upstate New York has had the ability to lure people from near and far. Many who settle here, like us, don't have family in the area, so "Friendsgiving" (sharing the Thanksgiving holiday with an ad hoc "family") has become a new tradition. Whether it's five people or forty, we find room for everyone at the table—and everyone's favorite dish.

It wouldn't be a Beekman 1802 cookbook if we didn't put a modern twist on the most traditional recipe of all: the holiday turkey. The flavors in this version are loosely inspired by the turkey club sandwich.

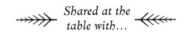

Shared at the table with…

Starting a day before serving, first make the marinade. In a bowl, whisk together the oil, poultry seasoning, salt, paprika, pepper, and garlic. Transfer half of the mixture to a jar and set aside.

Now start on the turkey. Rinse the turkey under cold running water and pat dry with paper towels. Run your fingers under the breast skin and carefully separate it from the flesh. Once the skin is loosened, dip your fingers into the remaining half of the marinade and rub it onto the breast meat under the skin. Place the thyme sprigs under the skin. Rub some marinade on the inside cavity of the turkey.

Continued

Club Roast Turkey

CONTINUED

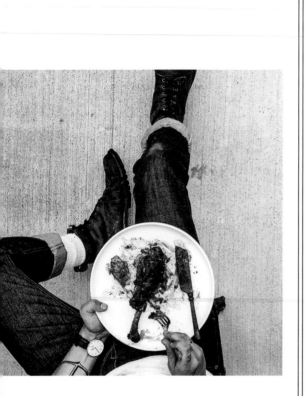

Place the turkey on a baking sheet and sprinkle the outside with the salt. Leave uncovered in the refrigerator overnight.

Take the turkey out of the refrigerator 2 hours before roasting and place it breast side up on a wire rack in a shallow, foil-covered roasting pan. Rub the reserved marinade from the jar all over the turkey. Place the onion, celery, parsley, and lemon in the cavity of the bird. Cover the breast and legs with bacon. Let the turkey come to room temperature—about 1 hour.

Meanwhile, preheat the oven to 400°F. Roast the turkey for 30 minutes. Lower the oven temperature to 350°F and roast for 2 more hours. Baste the turkey with drippings a few times during roasting. After the first hour, turn the turkey pan in the oven to ensure even browning. Use an instant-read thermometer to check the temperature of the turkey; take the bird out of the oven when a thermometer inserted into the inside of the thigh registers 165°F.

Lift the turkey from the roasting pan and transfer to a serving platter. Cover loosely with foil and let it rest for 30 minutes before carving. The bird will continue to cook as it rests.

Meanwhile, prepare the sauce. In a food processor pulse the yogurt, sour cream, dill, parsley, basil, garlic, lemon juice, and salt and pepper to taste; purée until well blended. Transfer the sauce to a serving bowl. Cover with plastic wrap. Refrigerate until ready to use.

Carve the bird. Serve the slices with a dollop of yogurt sauce or pass the sauce around as you would a bowl of gravy.

Fire pit -
Potato dogs

Fire-Pit Grilled Sausages and Potatoes

MAKES 4 SERVINGS

4 russet (baking) potatoes

1 tablespoon olive oil

½ teaspoon kosher salt

1 pound sweet Italian sausages

Start a fire with plenty of dry wood. Once your coals are ready, place your grill about 6 inches from the coals. Wash and dry the potatoes. Prick the potatoes all over with a fork. Rub them with oil and sprinkle with salt. Wrap them in a double layer of heavy duty aluminum foil. Bury the potatoes in the hot coals and cook for 45 minutes or until tender.

Grill the sausages for 10 to 15 minutes per side, turning them from time to time until cooked through.

Slice the potatoes lengthwise as shown on the next page and lay in the sausages.

When Rose Marie first bought her property in Sharon Springs, her family camped out with tents near the pond. They also entertained other family and friends who camped out with them. The kids always looked forward to having a big campfire, but Rose Marie looked forward to cooking over the beautiful hot coals. One fire-grilled favorite is Italian sausages; once the coals turn white, they are the perfect temperature to cook sausages and potatoes. Here the potatoes are used to serve the sausages and they capture the meat juices deliciously.

Do you like backyard camping, too? For a breakfast treat, bury some potatoes at the end of the campfire. They'll slowly cook and then cool overnight. You can use them to make home fry potatoes when you get your fire going again in the morning.

>>>→ *Shared at the table with…* ←<<<

_____

_____

_____

_____

Fried Chicken Cutlets
with Egg and Arugula

MAKES 4 SERVINGS

*When plating this simple recipe, you can
decide which comes first—the chicken or
the egg. Place the egg either underneath
or atop the cutlet.*

*Gratitude can transform
common days into thanks-
givings, turn routine jobs into
joy, and change ordinary
opportunities into blessings.*

William Arthur Ward

1 pound chicken cutlets

2 ounces grated
Pecorino Romano cheese
(about ½ cup)

½ teaspoon garlic
powder

3 tablespoons chopped
fresh parsley

2 large eggs, for the
batter

Salt and pepper

1 cup Italian-style
breadcrumbs

Oil for frying

2 cups baby arugula

4 small to medium eggs,
for serving

With a meat mallet, pound the cutlets to about ¼-inch
thickness. In a small, shallow bowl, stir together the cheese,
garlic powder, and parsley. In another shallow bowl, beat
the 2 large eggs and season with salt and pepper to taste.
Place the breadcrumbs in a third bowl. Dredge the cutlets
in the cheese mixture, then in the egg mixture, and then
finish with the breadcrumbs; be sure to coat both sides in
each bowl of coating.

In a large skillet, heat enough oil over medium heat to
sauté the chicken; cook until golden—3 to 5 minutes on
each side, depending on the thickness of the cutlet. Drain
on paper towels.

While the cutlets are draining, wipe out the pan to remove
any bits of the chicken but leave a coating of oil. Fry one
egg for each serving. We like to leave the yolks a little
runny so that they almost become a creamy sauce for the
dish, which takes about 5 minutes. As you fry eggs, use
additional oil to coat the skillet if necessary.

Arrange some arugula on a plate and top with a cutlet and
a fried egg—or a fried egg and a cutlet.

Chicken Drumsticks in Wine

MAKES 4 SERVINGS

¼ cup olive oil	1 bay leaf
8 chicken legs	1 small sprig rosemary
¼ cup all-purpose flour	¼ cup tomato paste
Salt and pepper	1 cup white wine
1 clove garlic, smashed	1 cup chicken broth

In a large sauté pan, heat the oil over medium heat. Toss chicken into a resealable plastic bag with flour, and salt and pepper to taste; shake to coat. Cook the chicken until golden brown—about 5 minutes per side. Turn the chicken often so that it browns evenly. Add the garlic, bay leaf, and rosemary and cook until the garlic is fragrant—5 to 7 minutes.

Add the tomato paste, stir it into the oil in the sauté pan, and cook for 1 minute. Add the wine and increase the heat to bring to a boil. Let boil for a few more minutes. Add the broth and reduce heat to low. Partially cover the pan and simmer until the meat is tender and sauce is thickened—45 minutes. Remove bay leaf.

Note: This is wonderful served over brown rice, with a starchy side or a big hunk of bread to sop up the delicious sauce.

As home cooks, we strongly believe that you don't need a pantry stocked with fancy ingredients. Living in the middle of nowhere has taught us that simplicity really is the new luxury, and that gratitude turns what we have into enough. The simplest ingredients, when combined expertly, are what creates an heirloom recipe that you'll make time and time again. And the memories built around the table that serves it? Those are priceless.

>>>> *Shared at the table with…* <<<<

_____

_____

_____

_____

_____

Crusted Lobster with Oregano Butter

MAKES 2 SERVINGS

6 tablespoons butter

5 tablespoons olive oil

¼ cup finely chopped fresh parsley

2 teaspoons dried oregano

2 tablespoons Dijon mustard

½ teaspoon salt

⅛ teaspoon red pepper flakes

Two 1¼-pound live lobsters

½ cup panko breadcrumbs

Even if they're being caught right outside your back door, lobster is still an extravagant delicacy. It's easy to prepare and has a beautiful taste all on its own, so when we splurge and buy a couple, we like to keep the preparation clean and simple.

Preheat the oven to 400°F. Line a shallow baking pan—large enough to hold the halved lobsters in a single layer—with heavy-duty foil.

In a small saucepan, heat the butter, 3 tablespoons of the oil, the parsley, oregano, mustard, salt, and pepper flakes over medium heat, stirring until the butter has melted. Set aside.

Split lobsters in half lengthwise. (You can also ask your fishmonger to do this for you when you buy the lobster.)

Place lobster halves cut side up on in the baking pan. Spoon the butter mixture evenly on the lobster halves and top with breadcrumbs. Drizzle the remaining 2 tablespoons of oil over the breadcrumbs. Bake until the flesh is firm and white and starts to pull away from the shell—12 to 14 minutes.

Note: In the warmer months, we like to serve this with boiled potatoes or corn on the cob—a simple meal that tastes of summer.

>>>> *Shared at the table with…* <<<<

Mussels with Breadcrumbs

MAKES 4 SERVINGS

When shopping for fresh mussels, look for shiny ones that are kept under and over ice. Dry, dull shells are a good indicator that the mussels are in a dying stage. When you bring the mussels home, store them in a bowl in the refrigerator covered with wet paper towels until you are ready to clean them. Wash the mussels in a colander under cold running water and scrub them if necessary.

Shared at the table with…

4 slices white sandwich bread, cubed

1 bunch fresh parsley, stems removed (about 2 cups)

2 large garlic cloves, peeled

1 teaspoon red pepper flakes

¼ teaspoon kosher salt

¼ teaspoon black pepper

½ cup grated Pecorino Romano cheese

½ cup olive oil

1 pound mussels, cleaned and debearded

½ cup white wine

Preheat the oven to 425°F. Line a rimmed baking sheet with heavy-duty foil.

In a food processor, pulse the bread, parsley, garlic, pepper flakes, salt, pepper, cheese, and oil until ingredients are roughly chopped and blended. The breadcrumbs should be coarse and moist.

In a large saucepan, heat the mussels and wine over medium-high heat. Cover and steam the mussels, removing them from the pan as they open—approximately 7 minutes after covering. Discard any unopened mussels. Of the opened mussels, remove top shells and discard. Arrange mussels on the baking sheet, shelled side up, and top each mussel with the breadcrumbs.

Bake 8 to 10 minutes or until the breadcrumbs are nicely browned.

Scallops Limoncello

10 sea scallops

¼ cup limoncello

Zest and juice of half a lemon

¼ cup white wine (like Moscato)

1 tablespoon olive oil

1 tablespoon butter

1 shallot, minced

1 garlic clove, minced

2 tablespoons chopped fresh parsley

1 slice prosciutto, coarsely chopped

Salt and pepper

1 tablespoon panko breadcrumbs

Move a shelf to the top position in the oven and preheat the oven to 425°F.

Make sure the scallops are dry. Place them in a baking dish and pour the limoncello, lemon juice, lemon zest, and wine over them.

In a small skillet, heat the oil and butter over medium-low heat. Add the shallot and garlic and cook, stirring occasionally, until golden. Remove from the heat and add the parsley and prosciutto. Spoon this mixture over the scallops and season with salt and pepper to taste. Sprinkle with breadcrumbs. Bake 12 minutes until breadcrumbs are golden and scallops are cooked through.

Note: Scallop half-shells make lovely serving dishes. Collect them during your next walk along the shore.

Limoncello is a lemon-based liqueur that is wonderful when used in a sauce for seafood. In this dish we've paired it with a white wine that's a little on the sweet side, but you could use any white wine that you have on hand—even a bottle from the previous night that you didn't quite finish.

>>>→ *Shared at the table with…* ←<<<

_____

_____

_____

_____

JASMINE CROWE

FOR SO MANY YEARS, young people—even those with strong roots in our area—have grown up and moved away from upstate New York.

There were no jobs, no opportunities, and no reason for them to stay.

But things are changing.

Jasmine is a member of the Beekman 1802 Rural Artisan Collective. She creates beautiful hand-thrown plates, bowls, and cups for the Mercantile. Her husband owns a feed company that supplies many of the local farmers.

Nothing puts a smile on our faces more than when Jasmine drops off her latest ceramics, assisted by her two children. The face of every child is like a crystal ball. You can see the future in it.

We hope that by the time Jasmine's kids are grown and ready to move away, they won't. Or their kids, as well.

We'll make more room at the table.

Sweet Ravioli with Ricotta and Honey

MAKES 15 RAVIOLI

When you live in the middle of nowhere and many miles from the nearest grocery store, you think long and hard before you throw anything away. Brent made these ravioli to use up leftover sweet ricotta filling. They are great to serve as a dessert or as a fun breakfast alternative to pancakes or French toast.

→→→→→ *Shared at the table with…* ←←←←←

_____

_____

_____

_____

SWEEET RICOTTA CREAM FILLING

1 cup ricotta

¼ cup confectioners' sugar

1 tablespoon mini chocolate chips

⅛ teaspoon finely grated lemon zest

⅛ teaspoon vanilla extract

30 wonton or dumpling wrappers

Butter for frying

Honey for garnish

The night before serving, line a colander with dampened cheesecloth and set over a bowl. Place ricotta in the colander; refrigerate and drain overnight. Transfer to a bowl, add the sugar, chocolate chips, zest, and vanilla and mix together.

Place a tablespoon of ricotta filling on the center of a wonton wrapper. Moisten the edges with water and cover with another wonton wrapper, pressing to release any air bubbles and to seal. Cut out circles with a raviolo cutter. You may also use a cookie cutter or glass as a guide and cut around the shape with a pastry wheel.

In a large nonstick skillet, melt a tablespoon of butter over medium-high heat. Cook 2 to 3 ravioli at a time so as not to crowd the pan until golden on both sides. Continue frying the remaining ravioli, adding more butter as you need it until all the ravioli are cooked.

Transfer to serving plates and drizzle with honey while still warm.

Salvation Chocolate Mousse Cake

MAKES 12 SERVINGS

This was Josh's birthday cake several years ago. Everyone was singing happy birthday, and as the cake was just about to be placed on the table in front of him, the entire cake slid off the platter right into Josh's hands—a miraculous save! This recipe calls for ladyfingers; you can buy these, 12 ladyfingers to a package, in the bakery department of most supermarkets.

>>>>>> *Shared at the* <<<<<
table with...

Three 3-ounce packages soft ladyfingers (you will need about 30 ladyfingers)

One 12-ounce package chocolate chips

1 teaspoon vegetable oil

2 cups heavy cream

4 tablespoons sugar

6 large eggs, separated

1 cup heavy cream, for serving (optional)

Open the ladyfingers along the long edge and use to line the bottom and sides of a 10-inch springform pan with a removable bottom (about 10 for the sides and 10 for each layer). You'll need to break a few ladyfingers to fill in gaps on the bottom layer to completely cover.

Place the chocolate chips and oil in a metal bowl set over a saucepan of barely simmering water. Melt the chocolate chips, stirring until smooth. Remove from heat, but keep the chocolate over the hot water; set aside. In a medium bowl, whip the cream with 2 tablespoons of sugar until soft peaks form.

In a large bowl, beat egg yolks and remaining 2 tablespoons sugar with a fork until combined. Add melted chocolate and mix well.

In a large bowl, beat egg whites until stiff peaks form. Gently fold egg whites into chocolate mixture. Fold in whipped cream. Pour half the mixture into the lined pan and add a layer of ladyfingers on top to form a middle layer. Pour the remaining filling into the pan. Cover with foil and refrigerate to set—6 hours or overnight.

To serve, release the sides of the pan and remove. If you like, whip 1 cup of heavy cream and either decorate the cake, or serve it in a bowl with the cake.

Note

You can make a gorgeous presentation by serving this cake with chocolate-dipped strawberries placed around the cake. Or if you don't want to make the whole cake but still want to serve an elegant dessert, just make the mousse filling. Fill wide champagne glasses with the mousse and serve with whipped cream and a cookie.

You may bake this batter
in six small Bundt cake
pans, as in the photo, for
about 18 minutes or until
a wooden pick inserted
in the cake comes out
clean. Follow the same
instructions for drizzling
with amaretto icing.

Boozy Bundt Cake

BUNDT CAKE

½ cup sliced almonds

1 ¼ cups unbleached all-purpose flour

1 cup cake flour

½ cup ground almond meal

1 tablespoon baking powder

1 teaspoon baking soda

½ teaspoon kosher salt

1 stick (4 ounces) unsalted butter, room temperature

1½ cups granulated sugar

3 large eggs

1 cup milk

¼ teaspoon almond extract

1 teaspoon vanilla extract

2 tablespoons amaretto liqueur

AMARETTO ICING

1 cup confectioners' sugar

½ cup amaretto liqueur

Preheat the oven to 350°F. Grease a 12-cup Bundt pan well. Scatter the sliced almonds in the pan, tilting to evenly distribute them around the bottom and sides.

In a bowl, stir together the flours, almond meal, baking powder, baking soda, and salt.

In another large bowl with an electric mixer on medium speed, beat butter and sugar until they are well mixed and resemble moist crumbles. Add the eggs, one at a time, beating well after each addition. Mix in milk, extracts, and amaretto. Scrape down the sides of the bowl with a spatula. With mixer on low speed, add the flour mixture in thirds and scrape down the sides of the bowl after each addition. Increase speed to medium-high and mix for 2 minutes. Pour batter into the prepared pan and bake for 50 minutes, until a wooden pick inserted in the cake comes out clean.

Continued

Megan had a weekend home in Sharon Springs several years before fate brought us here. As the farm and company started to grow (but before Josh could move to the farm full time), Brent needed a "right hand" to help. Using his sweet Southern charm, he convinced Megan to make a permanent move from New Jersey. (And after all these years she's still talking to us!) One Christmas she was overly generous with the brandy in a tiramisu, and Brent has never let her forget it. Now no matter what she cooks Brent jokingly asks her how much booze is in it. Megan will always have a seat at the table—even if she doesn't bring a drop of the good stuff.

Amaretto is an almond-based Italian liqueur that's often served as a cordial. This recipe incorporates the delightful taste of the liqueur into the cake. Megan, of course, loves it.

>>> *Shared at the table with...* <<<

Boozy Bundt Cake

Mix confectioners' sugar and amaretto in a measuring cup until smooth. Place the cake pan on a rack, and with a skewer poke holes into the cake about 1 inch apart. Drizzle icing slowly on cake, allowing it to soak in before adding more. Allow icing to soak in for 30 minutes, and then run a knife around the edge of the pan, if necessary, to separate the cake from the pan. Invert the cake onto a serving plate and allow to cool completely before serving.

ESPRESSO
COFFEE FOR ONE

A good espresso doesn't only have to taste good; it should also have a frothy foam, called *crema*. You don't have to own an expensive espresso machine to make a frothy cup of espresso.

Pour the first drops of espresso coffee, as it comes out of an espresso coffeepot, into a small bowl. Add enough sugar to thicken the coffee. Mix the coffee and sugar vigorously with a spoon until the coffee is caramel colored with a creamy, frothy consistency. When the mixture reaches the desired frothy consistency, pour one demitasse spoon of this mixture into an espresso cup and add the coffee from the pot. Stir gently; the coveted *crema* will form at the top of the cup.

One Perfect Mouthful Taralle Cookies

MAKES 64 COOKIES

COOKIES

½ cup milk

1 cup sugar

1 tablespoon vanilla extract

4 cups all-purpose flour

1 tablespoon baking powder

1 teaspoon salt

¾ cup vegetable shortening

4 large eggs, lightly beaten

LEMON ICING

2 large egg whites

2 tablespoons fresh lemon juice

1 teaspoon lemon extract

2 cups confectioners' sugar

Sprinkles for garnish

Light and lemony and bite-sized, taralle are Rose Marie's huband Joe's favorite Italian cookies. He especially enjoys them during the Christmas season when Rose Marie makes a large batch to share with friends and neighbors. When fresh, they are somewhat soft, but they keep well and can be enjoyed long after the holidays are over.

Shared at the table with…

Move an oven rack to the middle position and preheat the oven to 400°F. Line two cookie sheets with parchment.

In a small saucepan, heat milk and sugar and cook until sugar dissolves. Cool to room temperature, and then add the vanilla.

In a large mixing bowl, stir together the flour, baking powder, and salt. With your hands, work the shortening into the flour mixture until well blended. (Alternatively, you may use a pastry cutter instead of your hands.) Add the eggs to the flour mixture, using a fork to combine. Add the cooled milk mixture and mix with your hands until you have a smooth dough. Place the dough on a lightly floured wooden cutting board and shape into an even rectangle roughly 6 inches long, 4 inches wide, and 1½ inches high. Cut into 4 equal pieces. Cut each piece into 16 pieces and roll each to an 8-inch rope. Bring the ends together and twist into a circle. Place on cookie sheets.

Continued

One Perfect Mouthful Taralle Cookies

CONTINUED

Bake until golden—15 to 20 minutes. Transfer the cookies to a wire rack to cool completely.

Meanwhile, make the icing. In a small bowl, beat egg whites with lemon juice, lemon extract, and sugar until smooth. Dip cooled cookies in icing and garnish with sprinkles. Let dry and store in cookie tins.

PART TWO

WINTER

Many Mini Arancine

MAKES 24 TO 30 RICE BALLS, DEPENDING ON THE SIZE

Arancine *means "little oranges" in Sicilian, and these delicious rice balls are served as a street food throughout Sicily. With his first bite, Brent fell madly in love with both arancine and Rose Marie. When serving as an hors d'oeuvre, skewer with a cocktail pick or a small fork.*

>>>> *Shared at the table with…* <<<<

RISOTTO

Two 1-inch square chicken bouillon cubes

Salt

2 tablespoons butter

2 tablespoons olive oil

1 pound arborio rice

1/8 teaspoon saffron

1/2 cup grated Parmigiano cheese

1 large egg

BATTER FOR COATING

1/4 cup flour

1/8 teaspoon salt

1 large egg

24 small cubes of mozzarella (about the size of a marble)

Optional fillings to add to the mozzarella can include diced ham or prosciutto, meat ragu with peas, sautéed mushrooms, or whatever you have on hand and want to try

2 cups Italian-style breadcrumbs

4 cups vegetable oil for frying

First, make the risotto. In a 3-quart saucepan, bring 8 cups water and the bouillon to a simmer. Stir to dissolve the bouillon and make a broth; keep the broth warm on a very low flame. (Alternatively, you can substitute 8 cups chicken stock for the water and bouillon.) Taste and add salt if needed.

In a large heavy saucepan, melt 1 tablespoon butter; add the olive oil and the rice and stir until the grains are shiny and well coated. Stir in the warm broth by the ladleful and wait until each ladleful of broth is absorbed before adding more. Add the saffron when the risotto has cooked for about 15 minutes. Continue to add broth until rice is smooth and creamy, but still al dente—20 to 25 minutes. There may be some broth left over. Add the remaining butter and the

Continued

Many Mini Arancine

Parmigiano cheese and stir to blend well. Remove 2 cups of this rice and set aside for a risotto meal (use the leftover broth to thin it out). Pour the rest of the risotto onto a rimmed baking sheet, spread out evenly, and let cool. In a large bowl, beat the egg and add the cooled risotto. Mix well.

Now make the batter. In a small bowl, whisk together the flour, ¼ cup water, and the salt until smooth. Add the egg and whisk until well blended; set aside.

To form the balls, moisten your hands with water and place a tablespoon of risotto in the palm of your hand. Place a cube of mozzarella in the center of the risotto and cover with another tablespoon of rice. If you are using additional fillings, add a bit with the mozzarella before topping with the second tablespoon of rice. Shape into a ball using firm pressure. Place each shaped ball back on the baking sheet.

To coat the rice balls, pour the breadcrumbs into a shallow bowl. Using one hand for dry ingredients, and one for wet ingredients, dip each rice ball into the batter, and then into the breadcrumbs to coat thoroughly. After all of the rice balls are coated in breadcrumbs, it's time to fry them.

To deep fry the rice balls, heat the oil in a deep fryer or small pot to 375°F. Use a slotted metal spoon, to lower rice balls into the oil. Fry about 4 balls at a time until golden— approximately 4 minutes. Don't overcrowd the pan, which can lower the oil temperature, making the rice balls soggy. Drain the rice balls on paper towels and serve.

Bacon-Wrapped Stuffed Dates

MAKES 12 APPETIZERS

12 large pitted dates

12 small pieces
Parmigiano cheese

6 slices bacon, halved
crosswise

Preheat the oven to 375°F. Cut a slit in each date and fill
with a piece of Parmigiano cheese. Close the date, roll
a piece of bacon around it, and secure with a toothpick.
Arrange on a rimmed baking sheet lined with foil. Bake
until bacon is crispy—15 to 20 minutes depending on the
thickness of your bacon.

Many local craftspeople have contributed to the restoration and upkeep of the Beekman Farm over the years. One of them is Michael Whaling. He built the stone wall around the garden completely by hand, using no mechanical equipment; he used only a fulcrum and some ancient physics to move stones that weighed more than 500 pounds. The project took him more than a year to complete but was so worth the work when you think that the wall may very well be there 1,000 years from now.

Michael, we think you'd like these delicious (and easy) little treats. Come have a seat at our table.

>>>>> *Shared at the table with...* <<<<<

Zucchini Blossom Squares

MAKES 12 SERVINGS

Zucchini blossoms were one of the first things Rose Marie learned to cook. Her mom would pluck the blossoms, dip them in beaten egg and Italian breadcrumbs, and fry them for a delicious summer snack. Since that time, Rose Marie has become a little more creative with this seasonal bounty.

These zucchini blossom squares can be made ahead, frozen, and reheated. You'll always be prepared for a spontaneous gathering of friends and neighbors. To reheat, preheat the oven to 325°F. Place the frozen squares directly in the oven; don't thaw them, or they might get soggy. Bake for 15 minutes or until the center of the square is thawed.

>>>>>>————— *Shared at the table with…* —————<<<<<<

_____

_____

_____

_____

The only way to have a friend is to be one.

—Ralph Waldo Emerson

Olive oil cooking spray

1 recipe Pie Crust (page 118)

6 slices Genoa salami, chopped

2 small zucchini, thinly sliced

24 zucchini blossoms

1 cup pancake mix

2 cups milk

4 large eggs

½ teaspoon salt

¼ teaspoon pepper

1 onion, diced small

1 cup shredded Cheddar cheese

½ cup chopped fresh basil

Move an oven rack to the lowest position and preheat the oven to 350°F. Spray a 9- by 13-inch baking pan with olive oil cooking spray. Roll out the crust to fit the pan. Line the pan with the crust. (You can also make 12 individual squares as pictured.)

Scatter salami and zucchini over the crust. Arrange zucchini blossoms in rows, end to end until crust is covered (it is fine if they overlap).

In a large bowl whisk together the pancake mix, milk, eggs, salt, and pepper until well combined. Stir in the onion, cheese, and basil until combined and pour it over the blossoms. Bake 45 minutes or until golden brown and set. Transfer to a wire rack to cool for 10 minutes before cutting into squares.

Note

You may also add pieces of mild
cubed cheese such as provolone,
scamorza, or mozzarella.

Olive Salad

1 quart mixed olives (such as Sicilian green or Kalamata), pitted

One 7.5-ounce jar marinated artichokes, drained and quartered

One 12-ounce jar roasted red peppers, drained and cut into strips

3 stalks celery, thinly sliced

½ cup tender celery leaves

1 garlic clove, minced

½ small red onion, thinly sliced

1 teaspoon dried oregano

1 small hot pepper, chopped (you can substitute a pinch of red pepper flakes)

¼ cup roughly chopped fresh Italian parsley

2 tablespoons white wine vinegar

½ cup extra-virgin olive oil

Place all ingredients in a large bowl and mix well. Serve at room temperature.

Joe Todd is a small business owner with a notions shop right on Main Street in Sharon Springs. When we first came up with the idea of starting an annual Harvest Festival, JT (as we like to call him), immediately took on the responsibility of, well, virtually everything. Even as our little street festival has grown from 500 to 15,000 "neighbors" coming from around the world, JT still coordinates every single vendor. It's people like him who make any community work, and for that he will always have a seat at the table.

This salad uses the olive and not the proverbial olive branch, but we think it will get the same outcome.

Shared at the table with...

_____

_____

_____

_____

89

Fruit of the Sea Salad

MAKES 6 TO 8 SERVINGS

In Rose Marie's house, this is a must-have course for Christmas Eve dinner as part of the traditional "Feast of the Seven Fishes," but it is an excellent summer salad as well. It's great with the No-Knead Italian Bread on page 22.

If you have a hard time finding fresh seafood in your area, look in your supermarket's freezer section for "frozen seafood medley."

>>>>> *Shared at the table with...* <<<<<

1 pound frozen "heat and serve" mussels

12 little neck clams, soaked, scrubbed, and rinsed

2 tablespoon white vinegar

1 teaspoon kosher salt

1 tablespoon Old Bay seasoning

½ pound bay scallops

12 large raw shrimp, unpeeled

2 lobster tails

One 4-ounce can octopus in olive oil

½ cup extra-virgin olive oil

Juice of 2 lemons

Zest and juice of 1 tangerine

12 green olives, pitted and quartered

2 roasted red peppers, cut into strips

1 cup sliced celery with some leaves attached

1 small red onion, thinly sliced

1 large garlic clove, minced

¼ cup finely chopped fresh Italian parsley

½ teaspoon dried oregano

½ teaspoon red pepper flakes

Salt and pepper

Heat the mussels in a covered pan over high heat. (If you chose to use fresh mussels instead of frozen, add ½ cup white wine to the pan.) Remove mussels as they open and set them aside in a bowl. Discard any unopened mussels. After the mussels are all cooked (about 5 to 7 minutes, depending on the strength of heat), add clams to the pan and cover with a lid. Cook, shaking the pan from time to time. Remove the clams as they open and set in the bowl. Strain the pan juices and reserve ¼ cup. Shell the mussels and clams and transfer the seafood to a large bowl.

Continued

CONTINUED

In a 3-quart pot, bring 3 cups water, the vinegar, kosher salt, and Old Bay to a boil. Place the scallops in a mesh colander and submerge in the liquid for 2 minutes. Lift them out, drain, and add to the bowl with the mussels and clams.

Now add shrimp to the boiling water and cook until they turn pink—2 minutes. Lift out and cool. Add the lobster tails and cook until they turn bright red—8 minutes. Lift out and let cool. Peel the shrimp and add to the bowl with the seafood. Remove lobster meat from shells, cut into bite-sized chunks, and add to the bowl of seafood. Add the reserved pan juices, octopus, oil, lemon juice, tangerine juice and zest, olives, peppers, celery, onion, garlic, parsley, oregano, pepper flakes, and salt and pepper to taste; gently toss to mix. Taste and correct for salt.

Cover with plastic wrap and refrigerate at least 1 hour prior to serving to allow the flavors to come together. Bring to room temperature before serving.

Note: If your supermarket or fishmonger will steam the shellfish for you, you'll save a lot of time and effort. All you will have to do is mix the steamed seafood with the dressing.

Chick Pea Soup

MAKES 4 TO 6 SERVINGS

3 tablespoons olive oil

2 garlic cloves, smashed

¼ teaspoon red pepper flakes

3 tablespoons chopped fresh parsley

Two 15.5-ounce cans chick peas, rinsed and drained

1 teaspoon kosher salt

Pepper

Extra-virgin olive oil for drizzling (optional)

The vegetarians in your life will love you when you set this flavorful soup in front of them. Chick peas are packed with protein and make for a comforting cup of soup that truly serves as a meal.

>>>>> *Shared at the table with...* <<<<<

_____

_____

_____

_____

_____

In a large saucepan, heat the oil over low heat. Add the garlic and fry until golden—1 minute. Add pepper flakes, parsley, chick peas, salt, pepper to taste, and 6 cups of water. Increase heat to medium-high and bring to a boil. Lower the heat to medium, cover, and simmer 20 minutes. Remove half the chick peas and mash. Return the mashed chick peas to the saucepan and continue to simmer for 10 minutes. Taste and add more salt and pepper if necessary. Drizzle with olive oil.

Note: This recipe is so versatile. It is great as a soup alongside a hunk of bread or even with cooked pasta added at the end. You also can drain excess water and serve the chick peas as a side dish rather than a soup.

Sausage and Bean Soup

MAKES 6 SERVINGS

There are American, Hungarian, French, Portuguese, African, and Scandinavian variations of the story of Stone Soup—a parable that teaches how each of us can contribute a little to the whole, which then becomes something much greater than the sum of its parts. So many different cultures telling a similar story of neighborliness and gathering around a pot of soup is a lesson in and of itself.

Think of all the people in your community right now with whom you could share this wonderful recipe.

⟫⟫⟫ *Shared at the table with…* ⟪⟪⟪

_____

_____

_____

_____

2 tablespoons olive oil

1 large onion, chopped

½ pound Italian sausage, casings removed

3 garlic cloves, sliced

2 bay leaves

½ cup diced carrots

½ cup diced celery

1 large potato, peeled and diced

1 small zucchini, diced

4 cups chicken stock

Two 14.5-ounce cans cannellini beans, rinsed and drained

¼ cup chopped fresh parsley

One 2-inch-square piece Parmigiano cheese rind

½ pound small shell pasta

Grated Parmigiano cheese for serving at the table

In a large pot, heat oil over medium heat. Add onion and cook, stirring occasionally until softened—about 3 minutes. Add sausage, breaking it up with a wooden spoon, and cook until browned—about 5 minutes. Add garlic, bay leaves, carrots, celery, potato, zucchini, stock, beans, parsley, and cheese rind. Bring to a boil, and then reduce to a simmer. Cover and cook for 30 minutes; the stock will slightly thicken. Remove and discard bay leaves and cheese rind.

Meanwhile, cook pasta in salted water until al dente. Place ½ cup of pasta in each soup bowl and ladle soup over pasta. Serve with cheese.

Bacon Bread

MAKES 1 ROUND LOAF

William Beekman was orphaned at sea. Adopted in the colonies, he was a child soldier in the Revolutionary War. Without formal education, he became a successful businessman (opening the original Beekman Mercantile), a judge, and eventually a senator. He started building the namesake farmhouse in 1802. Sometimes we sit around our kitchen table and think about what it would have been like to break bread back in those days. Probably not too much different than what we do more than 200 years later.

Traditionally, this bread is made with pork cracklings (the crisp residue left after all the fat has been rendered). Here, we've used bacon because it's what we most often have on hand.

⇢⇢⇢ *Shared at the table with...* ⇠⇠⇠

1 teaspoon active dry yeast

1 tablespoon sugar

1 tablespoon olive oil

3 cups 00 flour

1½ teaspoons kosher salt

¼ pound bacon, cooked until crispy, and then crumbled

Freshly cracked pepper

Combine 1¼ cups water with yeast, sugar, and oil in a measuring cup with a pouring spout. Let stand 5 minutes or until foamy.

Combine flour and salt in a food processor; pulse a few times to mix. With the machine running, pour yeast mixture through the feed tube and pulse to combine. Add the bacon and cracked pepper to taste. Pulse a few times until the dough forms a ball. The bacon crumbles will still be visible. Place the dough in an oiled bowl and cover with plastic wrap. Let the dough rise in a warm, draft-free spot for 2 hours or until doubled in size.

Turn the dough onto a lightly floured board and divide into two equal pieces. Roll each piece into a thin long loaf about 18 inches long, making certain that there's a coating of flour on all sides. Twist the two loaves together and then bend into a circle. Place on an oiled pizza pan and cover with a cotton dish towel. Let rise for 2 hours. Meanwhile, move an oven rack to the middle position and preheat the oven to 425°F.

Bake 30 minutes or until the bread is golden brown. Place on a wire rack to cool.

Seasoned Breadcrumbs

MAKES 1 CUP BREADCRUMBS

4 slices white sandwich bread, cubed

1 bunch fresh parsley, stems removed

2 large garlic cloves, peeled

1 teaspoon red pepper flakes

¼ teaspoon salt

¼ teaspoon freshly ground black pepper

½ cup grated Pecorino Romano cheese

½ cup olive oil

Place bread in a food processor and pulse until you have coarse breadcrumbs. Transfer to a bowl. Add parsley and garlic to the food processor and pulse until finely chopped. Add to the bowl of breadcrumbs. Add the red pepper flakes, salt, black pepper, cheese, and oil and mix to combine.

If you are not using the crumbs immediately, store in an airtight container in the refrigerator for up to 1 week. You can also toast the mixture in a frying pan at medium heat with 2 tablespoons of olive oil, constantly stirring, until the crumbs are completely dry. Freeze or store in an airtight container for up to 1 month.

These breadcrumbs are wonderful as a topping for clams or fish fillets, or to fill mushrooms. Or try them in Mussels with Breadcrumbs (page 64).

Shared at the table with…

Mushrooms with Cream

MAKES 4 SERVINGS

These mushrooms are wonderful as a side dish with steak, or as a topping for pasta with the addition of a drizzle of truffle oil and a sprinkling of Parmigiano cheese.

>>>> *Shared at the table with...* <<<<

2 tablespoons butter

1 small onion, finely chopped

½ pound mushrooms, cut into ¼-inch slices

Salt and pepper

½ cup heavy cream

1 teaspoon all-purpose flour

In a large saucepan, melt butter over medium heat. Add onion and mushrooms, cover the pan, and turn heat on high until you see steam coming out of the pan. Uncover and let any excess liquid evaporate. Add salt and pepper to taste. Cook on high heat until both the mushrooms and onion are tender—about 5 minutes—stirring to prevent scorching. In a small bowl, whisk cream into flour. Add cream mixture to the pot and cook, stirring, until sauce is creamy—7 to 10 minutes

Blue Cheese Potato Slices

MAKES 4 SERVINGS

2 baking potatoes, baked and refrigerated until thoroughly cooled

½ cup blue cheese crumbles

3 tablespoons heavy cream

1 tablespoon chopped fresh chives

Move an oven rack to the middle position and preheat the oven to 425°F. Lightly oil a rimmed baking sheet.

Cut cold potatoes into ¼-inch-thick slices. Place potatoes on the baking sheet.

In a small bowl, mix together the cheese and cream and spoon it evenly over the potatoes.

Bake until hot—about 5 minutes. Transfer to a serving dish and sprinkle with chives.

If your family likes to have potatoes a couple of nights a week, here's a great way to think ahead when planning the week's meals. If you are having baked potatoes one night, throw a couple of extras in the oven. They'll keep in the refrigerator for several days, making them perfect for this roasted potato recipe that is ready in a flash.

⟶⟶⟶ *Shared at the table with…* ⟵⟵⟵

_____

_____

_____

_____

_____

Tomato, Olive, and Caper Sauce

MAKES 6 TO 8 SERVINGS

*Many people think they don't like ancho-
vies, but when the fish are "melted" into
this sauce, they provide a delicious saltiness
that makes this recipe taste more complex
and involved than it actually is. The sauce
is delicious spooned over grilled fish, or you
can add a pound of shrimp, cook for a few
minutes, and toss it with linguini.*

3 tablespoons olive oil

1 large onion, coarsely
chopped

2 garlic cloves, chopped

¼ teaspoon red pepper
flakes

3 anchovy fillets,
chopped

One 28-ounce can diced
tomatoes

¼ cup each black oil–
cured olives and green
olives, pitted and sliced

¼ cup capers, drained

½ teaspoon salt

½ cup chopped fresh
parsley

>>>> *Shared at the* <<<<
table with…

In a large saucepan, heat the oil over medium heat. Add
the onion and cook, stirring occasionally, until the onion
is translucent—7 minutes. Add the garlic and cook 1
minute. Add the pepper flakes and anchovies and stir
with a wooden spoon to dissolve the anchovies. Stir in the
tomatoes, cover, and simmer 10 minutes. Add the olives,
capers, salt, and ¼ cup of parsley. Cover and simmer
for 10 minutes until the flavors have blended. Stir in the
remaining ¼ cup parsley.

Your own safety is at stake when
your neighbor's house is in flames.

—Horace

MICHAEL McCARTHY

DEB McGILLYCUDDY WAS THE PERSON who first showed us how to make soap using our goat milk. Once we had our website up and running and started selling a few bars of soap, she asked us if we knew Karen Tenney.

Karen was a neighbor just down the street, and when we went to visit for the first time, we couldn't help but notice the antique loom in her living room. She became the very first member of the Beekman 1802 Rural Artisan Collective, and we still sell her hand-woven linens.

One day Karen asked if we had ever met Michael McCarthy, the blacksmith who lived in the next village over. How many villages still lay claim to their very own blacksmith? We decided we had to pay a visit.

Michael constructed his own forge, mines his own iron ore, chops all the wood that heats the forge, and can make pretty much anything you ask of him. He is an artist for sure, but stays in this small community because there's no one else for miles and miles around who can come to the rescue when the local farmers need a repair on their tractors.

On our first visit to the shop, we saw what looked like an old spoon mold. Michael said it was indeed such a mold and that it dated back to the late 1800s. We asked if he would consider firing up the forge and showing us how a spoon is made.

That spoon was the first product we made with Michael. Before we knew it, the spoon was featured in the *New York Times,* and overnight we had a waiting list for more than 1,000 of them. (And one of those spoons has been slyly featured in the photography of every single one of our prior cookbooks.)

We've kept Michael busy since then, making everything from candlesticks to furniture, and he's always welcome to our table.

And not just because he's made us one.

Poached Eggs in Tomato Sauce

MAKES 2 SERVINGS

If you've made a homemade sauce (or opened up a jar of the Beekman 1802 Mortgage Lifter sauce), then you know it's good to the last drop, so why waste it? Eggs simmered in tomato sauce is such a universal, international recipe that you can find variations in many cultures, such as Middle Eastern shakshuka.

⇢⇢⇢⇢ *Shared at the table with...* ⇠⇠⇠⇠

2 cups tomato sauce

4 large eggs

Salt and pepper

¼ cup grated Pecorino

Romano cheese

Basil leaves, torn into bite-size pieces, for garnish

In a large skillet, bring the sauce to a simmer over medium heat. Carefully crack the eggs into the simmering sauce, spacing evenly throughout the sauce and being careful not to break the yolks. The eggs should be nestled in the sauce but not submerged. Adjust heat to low. Cover the skillet and poach the eggs until the whites have solidified but the yolks are still runny—3 to 5 minutes. Season with salt and pepper to taste. Plate and garnish with cheese and basil.

Fennel Spice Rub

MAKES ABOUT ½ CUP RUB

2 tablespoons fennel
seeds

2 teaspoons red pepper
flakes

1 teaspoon black
peppercorns

2 tablespoons fresh
rosemary leaves, minced

4 garlic cloves, minced

Grated zest of 1 lemon

1 tablespoon sea salt

Toast the fennel seed, pepper flakes, and peppercorns in
a small skillet until fragrant—about 1 minute. Cool to
room temperature, then transfer to a mortar and pestle
and crush the seeds. Transfer to a bowl, add the rosemary,
garlic, lemon zest, and salt; blend. Store in a closed jar in
the refrigerator for up to 6 months

*This spice rub can be made ahead and
stored in the refrigerator. It's great to have
on hand for quick use as a rub on pork
roasts, ribs, and pork belly. It's also good
mixed with olive oil and lemon juice as a
marinade for fish or chicken.*

>>> *Shared at the
table with...* <<<

_____

_____

_____

_____

_____

Spaetzle

MAKES 4 SERVINGS

Spaetlze *means "little sparrow" but it's essentially a very fresh and easy-to-make pasta. Serve it as a side dish with meats (particularly those with a nice* jus), *or add other seasonings or spice blends to it to complement vegetables.*

We've served it up with our Veal Swiss Style from the next page, but the simple chive butter coating makes the spaetlze excellent alone as a light lunch.

>>>>> *Shared at the* <<<<<
table with…

_____

_____

_____

_____

For a photograph of this dish, turn the page

1 cup all-purpose flour	¼ cup milk
1 teaspoon salt	Cooking spray
½ teaspoon ground pepper	3 tablespoons unsalted butter
½ teaspoon ground nutmeg	2 tablespoons minced fresh chives
2 large eggs	Salt and pepper

In a large bowl, combine the flour, salt, pepper, and nutmeg. In another mixing bowl, whisk the eggs and milk together. Make a well in the center of the dry ingredients and pour in the egg-milk mixture. Using a fork, gradually draw in the flour from the sides and stir until well combined; the dough should be smooth and thick. Cover and let the dough rest for 10 to 15 minutes.

Bring 3 quarts of salted water to a boil in a large pot, and then reduce to a simmer. To form the spaetzle, spray a little cooking spray on a colander with large holes or a large-hole flat grater that is long enough that you can rest it atop the pot. Hold the colander or flat grater over the simmering water and push the dough through the holes with a spatula or spoon. Do this in batches so you don't overcrowd the pot. Cook for 1 to 2 minutes or until the spaetzle floats to the surface, stirring gently to prevent the pasta from sticking. Dump the spaetzle into a colander and give it a quick rinse with cool water.

In a large skillet, melt the butter over medium heat and add the spaetzle, tossing to coat. Cook the spaetzle for 1 to 2 minutes, until lightly browned, and then sprinkle with the minced chives. Season with salt and pepper to taste before serving.

Veal Swiss Style

MAKES 6 TO 8 SERVINGS

2 to 3 tablespoons all-purpose flour

2 pounds veal cutlets, sliced into ¾-inch-wide strips

4 tablespoons unsalted butter

2 tablespoons olive oil

1 medium onion, thinly sliced

2 garlic cloves, thinly sliced

15 fresh sage leaves, chopped

8 ounces mushrooms, thickly sliced

1 cup dry white wine

Salt and pepper

1¼ cups heavy cream

Sprinkle the flour over the meat and toss to coat. In a large skillet, heat 2 tablespoons of the butter and 1 tablespoon of the oil over medium-high heat. As soon as the butter foams, add the meat and brown it very quickly on all sides. Set aside on a plate.

Keeping the pan at medium heat, add the remaining 2 tablespoons butter and 1 tablespoon oil to the pan and cook the onion, garlic, and sage until the garlic is golden—3 minutes. Add the mushrooms, stir to coat, and cook until tender—5 minutes.

Add the wine to deglaze the bottom of the pan, using a wooden spoon to scrape up any browned bits. Add the veal back and cook, stirring, until the wine has evaporated. Reduce the heat to low and cook for another 10 minutes. The meat will continue to brown as it cooks through.

Season with salt and pepper to taste, add the cream, and let it bubble for 2 minutes. Remove from the heat and serve with a crusty bread or over spaetzle (recipe on previous page).

Paul and Phyllis and the rest of the Van Amburgh family own the farm that borders our own. Known as Dharma Lea, the farm raises organic beef and produces organic milk. When we need cow's milk to make butter or whipped cream, we just walk over and get some. After our challenging experiments raising our own cows for beef, we decided to leave it to the experts next door.

This recipe makes enough to feed an entire farm family, and the Van Amburghs always have a seat at our table.

>>>→ *Shared at the table with...* ←<<<

Spaetzle (page 108) with Veal Swiss Style (page 109)

Beef Chili Masala

MAKES 4 TO 6 SERVINGS

Garam masala is a blend of spices that you find in every Indian household, and you can easily find the blend in your neighborhood grocery store. This aromatic mixture usually contains black pepper, cardamom, cinnamon, cloves, coriander, nutmeg, and turmeric, and takes chili from ordinary to extraordinary. Serve this flavorful chili with basmati rice, lime wedges, yogurt, and chopped cilantro.

⟩⟩⟩ *Shared at the table with...* ⟨⟨⟨

_____

_____

_____

_____

½ teaspoon red chili powder

½ teaspoon turmeric

¼ teaspoon black pepper

1 teaspoon coriander seeds

½ teaspoon fennel seeds

¼ teaspoon cumin seeds

3 tablespoons butter

1 cup coarsely chopped onion

3 cloves garlic, mashed

1 quarter-size slice fresh ginger, mashed and chopped

1 scotch bonnet pepper (scotch bonnets are very hot!) or ½ teaspoon red pepper flakes

1 pound ground beef

One 14.5-ounce can petite diced tomatoes

1 cinnamon stick

1 star anise

1 teaspoon mango powder or the juice of a lime

1½ teaspoons salt

1 teaspoon white vinegar

3 small potatoes (any type you like), cut into small cubes (about 1½ cups)

½ cup frozen peas

1 teaspoon garam masala

1 tablespoon chopped fresh cilantro (or to taste)

In a large heavy-bottomed saucepan or Dutch oven, toast the chili powder, turmeric, black pepper, coriander seeds, fennel seeds, and cumin seeds at high heat until they begin to pop and are fragrant. Add the butter and onion and cook, stirring occasionally, until the onion is translucent—5 minutes. Add the garlic, ginger, and scotch bonnet pepper and cook until the garlic is golden.

Add the beef and stir with a wooden spoon to break up any lumps. Cook, stirring, until browned—about 10 minutes. Add 2 cups of water and the tomatoes, reduce heat to medium, and simmer for 10 minutes. Add the cinnamon stick, star anise, mango powder, salt, vinegar, and potatoes; increase heat to bring to a boil. Reduce to a simmer, cover, and cook until the beef is tender—30 minutes. Add the peas, garam masala, and cilantro and cook another 10 minutes. Taste and add more salt, if necessary. Remove cinnamon stick and star anise before serving.

Rib Eye Steak Palermo Style

Two 8-ounce rib eye steaks

Salt and pepper

Olive oil

1 garlic clove, minced

1 tablespoon chopped fresh parsley

Grated zest of half a lemon

2 chopped anchovies

1 teaspoon capers, drained

1 tablespoon grated Parmigiano cheese

¼ cup plain dry breadcrumbs

Despite writing cookbooks and tasting virtually any type of cuisine that is put in front of us, at heart we are just country boys who have grown into meat and potato men. This savory spin on rib eye steak is sure to satisfy any similar folks you happen to know.

>>> *Shared at the table with…* <<<

_____

_____

_____

_____

Preheat the oven to 325°F. Season steaks with salt and pepper to taste. Rub each steak with 1 teaspoon olive oil and set aside.

In a bowl, mix together garlic, parsley, lemon zest, anchovies, capers, cheese, and breadcrumbs. Add enough of the remaining oil to moisten the crumbs.

In a large cast-iron skillet, heat 1 teaspoon of the oil over medium-high heat and sear the steaks on one side for 3 minutes. Turn the steaks and pat the breadcrumb mixture over the steaks, pressing the crumbs to adhere. Place the skillet in the oven and roast the steaks 15 minutes for medium rare (roast longer to your desired degree of doneness) or until the breadcrumbs are golden brown. Slice and serve.

Crowded Meatballs

MAKES ABOUT 15 GOOD-SIZED MEATBALLS

This recipe is a true heirloom that was developed by Josh's godfather, tweaked by Josh's mom, and further personalized by us. We call it "crowded" because there's a lot of stuff in there, and a few of them can feed a crowd! You can also use this mixture as an alternative in the Stuffed Onions recipe (page 154).

>>>>> *Shared at the table with...* <<<<<

4 slices white bread, preferably stale, cut into ½-inch cubes

1 pound ground beef (or ½ pound pork, ½ pound beef)

2 eggs

½ cup Romano cheese (you can substitute Parmigiano or Beekman 1802 Blaak goat cheese)

4 tablespoons chopped fresh parsley or 2 tablespoons dried parsley

2 teaspoons garlic salt (more or less to your taste)

2 teaspoons fresh oregano leaves, finely chopped, or 1 teaspoon dried oregano

Salt and pepper, to taste

Preheat the oven to 400°F. Combine all ingredients in a large bowl and use your hands to mix thoroughly. Use your palms to roll individual meatballs 2 to 3 inches in diameter. Arrange the meatballs on a baking sheet with a rim. Bake meatballs for 15 to 20 minutes, or until the outsides are thoroughly browned. Transfer desired quantity to a simmering sauce, such as a marinara sauce, and cook at least another half hour, until meat is cooked all the way through.

Once cooked, the meatballs may also be frozen for later use. If you freeze the meatballs, allow them to partially thaw before throwing them into a simmering sauce or reheating in the oven or microwave.

Note: For a romantic *alla tavola* (right) for two, simply use your kitchen cutting board as your serving piece and share. One of you can be the lady and one of you can be the tramp.

PASTA ALLA TAVOLA

IN SICILY DURING HARVEST SEASON several families would gather in the countryside either to work on their land together or to celebrate the fall harvest. The women would set up outdoor kitchens and over an open fire cook huge pots of tomato sauce with meatballs, sausages, rabbit, or whatever meat they had on hand. Some would bring fresh pasta made that morning. These were the days before paper or plastic plates were locally available, and the women would never bring their precious plates from home for fear that they would break, so the people had to improvise. When it was time to eat, they'd place the cooked meats in the center of a large old millstone set on a stone pedestal, which had been thoroughly scrubbed clean and served as a table. They'd pour the pasta along the edges of the table surrounding the meat. Additional sauce was poured over the pasta and meat. Each person would take his or her place around the table and claim their section of pasta and meat. The entire group would eat together from the table with no plates. The men would use their pocketknives to fashion forks for the family out of wild bamboo. Wine was poured from wine pouches and drunk from tin cups. You had to be watchful of your portion of pasta and meat because your neighbor might jokingly try to "steal" some of your portion. If there was not enough room around the table, folks fashioned plates out of large prickly pear leaves from which the thorns were removed. A couple of the men brought guitars or accordions so there was music and singing to make the day even more festive.

To celebrate the creation of this cookbook, the entire team gathered for an *alla tavola* (meaning "on the table"). Rose Marie's husband whittled the forks. This photo was taken at the end of our first day of cooking.

Chicken Apricot Pot Pie

MAKES 6 TO 8 SERVINGS

During the months of January, February, and March at the farm, the daily temperatures huddle around 0°F and several feet of snow cover the ground. Even though we love winters on the farm, we'd be lying if we said our thoughts didn't occasionally drift to warmer, more exotic locales. This twist on a comfort food classic is a soul-satisfying vacation from those cold, short winter days.

>>>> *Shared at the table with...* <<<<

PIE CRUST

2 cups all-purpose flour

1 tablespoon sugar

¼ teaspoon salt

½ cup (8 tablespoons) cold unsalted butter, cut into cubes

2 tablespoons olive oil

5 tablespoons ice water

CHICKEN-APRICOT FILLING

2 tablespoons olive oil

1 large onion, finely chopped

1 garlic clove, finely chopped

1½ pounds boneless chicken breast, cut into 1-inch cubes

½ teaspoon salt

⅛ teaspoon black pepper

1 teaspoon ground cinnamon

1 teaspoon ground ginger

½ teaspoon turmeric

3 tablespoons fresh lemon juice

½ cup dried apricots

2 cups tomatoes, diced

¼ cup sliced almonds

¼ cup golden raisins

⅛ teaspoon crumbled saffron threads

2 cups low-sodium chicken broth or homemade stock

1 tablespoon orange flower water (or use ½ teaspoon orange zest as a substitute)

2 tablespoons chopped fresh cilantro

2 tablespoons chopped fresh Italian parsley

3 tablespoons butter

¼ cup all-purpose flour

Salt and pepper

First make the pie crust. In a large bowl, stir together the flour, sugar, and salt until combined. Using the large holes of a box grater, grate the cold butter into the flour mixture. Coat butter with flour as you grate. Add the oil and mix quickly with your hands. Add the water and bring dough

Continued

Chicken Apricot Pot Pie

CONTINUED

together. Shape into two disks and wrap each disk in plastic wrap. Refrigerate at least 30 minutes. You only use one disk for this recipe; to freeze the second disk for a future pot pie, wrap it well and freeze for up to several months.

Meanwhile, make the chicken-apricot filling. Preheat the oven to 425°F. In a large, heavy skillet, heat the oil over medium heat. Add the onion and cook, stirring occasionally, until translucent. Add the garlic and cook 3 minutes. Add chicken and cook until lightly browned—3 to 5 minutes. If your skillet is not large enough to cook the ingredients in a single layer without overlapping of the chicken, do this step in batches so that the chicken is browning.

Add the salt, pepper, cinnamon, ginger, and turmeric; cook, stirring, for 1 minute. Add the lemon juice, apricots, tomatoes, almonds, raisins, saffron, and broth. Increase the heat to high and bring to a boil, then quickly lower heat to a simmer. (If it starts to boil again, reduce heat further.) Cook uncovered until the chicken is cooked through—20 minutes. Remove from heat and add the orange flower water, cilantro, and parsley. Set skillet aside.

In a small saucepan, melt the butter over medium heat. Add the flour and stir until smooth. Add to the skillet and stir to combine. Place the skillet on medium heat and simmer until the sauce thickens and coats the chicken. Taste the filling and season with salt and pepper, if needed. Set aside to cool.

Meanwhile, as the filling is cooling, roll out pie crust large enough to cover a 9- by 13-inch casserole. Spoon the filling into a 9- by 13-inch glass casserole dish and cover with the rolled pie crust. Cut slits in several places on the crust.

Flute the edge of the crust by using the thumb of your right hand to push a bit of the dough between the space created when pinching the index finger and thumb of your left hand together.

Bake 30 to 40 minutes until the crust is golden brown.

Mussels with White Wine and Cream

MAKES 2 SERVINGS

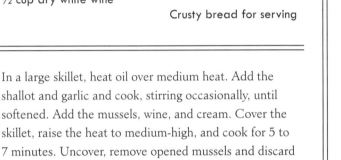

2 tablespoons olive oil

1 large shallot, minced

2 garlic cloves, minced

1 pound mussels, cleaned and debearded

½ cup dry white wine

¼ cup heavy cream

2 tablespoons unsalted butter

1 tablespoon chopped fresh parsley

Salt and pepper

Crusty bread for serving

In a large skillet, heat oil over medium heat. Add the shallot and garlic and cook, stirring occasionally, until softened. Add the mussels, wine, and cream. Cover the skillet, raise the heat to medium-high, and cook for 5 to 7 minutes. Uncover, remove opened mussels and discard unopened mussels. Return opened mussels to pan. Add butter, parsley, and salt and pepper to taste. Serve with chunks of crusty bread.

When Josh sees moules frites—the classic dish of mussels and fries—on a menu, he simply cannot resist. This comfort food was first served to him by his French uncle. While there are no fries with this take on mussels, the pan juices are so delicious you'll want an entire loaf of crusty bread for mopping them up. Pull your chair closer to the table. This is going to be juicy!

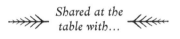

Shared at the table with…

The Devil's Stew

MAKES 4 SERVINGS

This delicious stew gets its name partially from the spicy heat of the red pepper flakes and partially because its motley components give the impression that you are staring into a cauldron of lost souls.

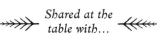

Shared at the table with...

½ pound linguine

3 tablespoons olive oil

2 garlic cloves, thinly sliced

24 mussels, cleaned and debearded

12 littleneck clams, well scrubbed

½ cup white wine

One 28-ounce can crushed tomatoes

1 teaspoon red pepper flakes

Salt and pepper

12 large shrimp, peeled and deveined

½ pound bay scallops

¼ cup chopped fresh parsley

In a large pot of boiling salted water, cook the linguine until al dente; drain.

Meanwhile, in a large skillet big enough to hold all the seafood and cooked pasta, heat the oil over medium heat. Add the garlic and cook until pale gold. Add mussels, clams, and white wine. Increase heat to medium-high; cover and cook for about 7 minutes. Check frequently; remove mussels and clams as they open; set aside. Discard any unopened shellfish. When all mussels and clams have opened or been removed, lower heat and add tomatoes, pepper flakes, and salt and pepper to taste. Cook about 15 minutes to let sauce thicken. Add the shrimp and scallops and cook until the shrimp turn pink. Return the mussels and clams to the skillet and lower heat to very low.

By this time the pasta should be cooked. Drain the pasta and add to the pan with the seafood. Sprinkle with parsley and toss to coat the pasta with the sauce.

Fig Cookies

MAKES 32 COOKIES

When Rose Marie was a child growing up in Sicily, the family seldom ate dessert. Dessert was a special homemade treat reserved for holidays or other special occasions. With her family's move to the United States, dessert took on a social function. When an Italian-American visits family or friends, it's customary to bring a box of bite-sized pastries. The host prepares espresso coffee (see page 76) and everyone enjoys the treats.

This recipe makes enough fig-filled cookies for every member of a big Italian family!

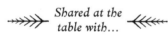
Shared at the table with...

_____

_____

_____

_____

FIG FILLING

½ cup walnuts

½ cup almonds

2 cups plump dried figs, stems removed

½ cup dark chocolate chips

¼ cup honey

¼ cup orange marmalade

1 teaspoon ground cinnamon

½ teaspoon ground cloves

Finely grated zest of 1 orange

DOUGH

4 cups all-purpose flour

4 teaspoons baking powder

1 teaspoon baking soda

¼ teaspoon salt

½ cup vegetable shortening

4 tablespoons cold butter, cut into small dice

½ cup milk

½ cup sugar

2 large eggs

1 tablespoon vanilla extract

FINISHING

1 large egg

Colored sprinkles (optional)

Confectioners' sugar for serving

Start by making the filling. Preheat the oven to 350°F. Place the walnuts and almonds on a baking sheet and bake until crisp and fragrant—about 7 minutes. In a food processor, pulse the figs until coarsely chopped. Add the toasted walnuts and almonds, chocolate chips, honey, orange marmalade, cinnamon, cloves, and orange zest and pulse until well combined. The filling will be moist.

Move an oven rack to the middle position and preheat the oven to 400°F.

Now make the dough. In a large bowl, mix together the flour, baking powder, baking soda, and salt. With a pastry blender, cut the shortening and butter into the flour mixture until it's the texture of coarse crumbs. With your hands, mix until well blended. In a small saucepan, heat the milk and sugar over low heat until the sugar dissolves. Add the milk mixture, eggs, and vanilla to the flour mixture and mix with a fork until the dough starts to come together. Place the dough on a lightly floured work surface and knead until smooth—about 5 minutes.

Divide the dough into 4 equal parts, and then cut each part into 8 equal pieces for a total of 32 pieces. Using the palm of your hand, flatten each piece into a 2 by 4-inch rectangle. Place a heaping teaspoon of filling in the center of the dough. Bring the edges together to enclose the filling and pinch together to seal. Roll each piece over so the seam is on the bottom and shape each cookie into a crescent shape, making sure that the filling is totally enclosed. With a very sharp knife or razor blade, cut 4 slits into each cookie on one side and fan the cuts open. Score small cuts on top of the cookie to decorate without cutting totally through the dough.

Place cookies 1 inch apart on a non-stick or parchment lined cookie sheet. In a small bowl, beat together the egg and 1 tablespoon water; use a pastry brush to brush the mixture over the cookies. If you like, you can sprinkle the cookies with colored sprinkles to make them look festive. Bake for 15 to 18 minutes, or until golden. Cool the cookies on the cookie sheet for 5 minutes, and then transfer to a wire rack to cool completely. Sprinkle with confectioners' sugar before serving.

St. Joseph's Day Cream Puffs

MAKES 16 TO 20 CREAM PUFFS

In Italy, St. Joseph is the patron saint of households and March 19th is not only his feast day, but also Father's Day. It's traditional in Sicily to share food with friends and neighbors on this day. In Rose Marie's hometown of Campofiorito, many families held open houses to share their food with the community. They would set up elaborate altars to honor the saint. Basically, the altar is a table with a statue of the saint in the middle surrounded by breads, vegetable dishes, fruits, and pastries. If your name is Joseph or Josephine, you typically receive St. Joseph's Day cards and are wished a happy name day. Because Rose Marie's husband is a Joseph, she follows this tradition by setting up an altar in her foyer and inviting friends over for dinner.

>>>> *Shared at the* <<<<
table with…

_____

_____

_____

_____

RICOTTA CREAM FILLING

1 pound ricotta cheese

¼ teaspoon vanilla extract

1 cup sugar (more or less to taste)

¼ cup shelled pistachios, coarsely chopped

¼ cup candied lemon peel, coarsely chopped

¼ cup semisweet mini chocolate chips

PASTRY

Cooking spray

8 tablespoons salted butter

¼ teaspoon salt

¼ teaspoon finely grated orange zest

1 cup all-purpose flour

4 large eggs

FINISHING

10 candied red cherries, halved (optional)

20 strips candied orange peel (optional)

Confectioners' sugar for serving

First, make the ricotta cream filling. Line a colander with dampened cheesecloth and set over a bowl. Place ricotta in the colander; refrigerate and drain overnight. Transfer ricotta to a large bowl and stir in the vanilla and sugar until completely mixed. Add the pistachios, lemon peel, and chocolate chips and mix together. Taste and correct for sweetness. Refrigerate until ready to use. It is best to fill the cream puffs just before serving.

Now make the pastry. Move an oven rack to the middle position and preheat the oven to 425°F. Spray a cookie sheet with cooking spray.

In a 3-quart saucepan, combine butter, 1 cup water, salt, and orange zest and cook over medium heat until the butter has melted.

Remove from the heat and add flour all at once. Stir with a wooden spoon until the dough forms a ball. Add eggs, one at a time, stirring each egg until well incorporated before adding another. The mixture will be shiny, and running a finger through it will leave a trench.

Drop dough by heaping tablespoons onto cookie sheet, spacing 2 inches apart. Bake 10 minutes, and then reduce to the oven temperature to 325°F and bake 15 minutes, or until golden and puffy. Remove the cream puffs from the cookie sheet and transfer to a wire rack to cool completely.

Using a small paring knife, slice along the middle of the cream puff without going completely through, forming a pocket for the filling. Fill the cream puff with the ricotta cream filling, letting it overflow a bit. Decorate with cherries and orange peel, if desired. Dust with confectioners' sugar and serve.

Almond Brittle

MAKES ABOUT ¾ POUND BRITTLE

Cooking spray

½ pound (2 cups) natural almonds

¾ cup sugar

¼ cup honey

Finely grated orange zest from half an orange

½ lemon

Preheat the oven to 350°F. Spray a cookie sheet with cooking spray.

Place almonds on a baking sheet and toast until crisp and fragrant—about 10 minutes.

In a large nonstick skillet, heat sugar, honey, ¼ cup water, and the orange zest over medium heat, stirring until the sugar dissolves and the mixture is a deep golden caramel color—8 to 10 minutes. Raise the heat to medium-high and continue to cook until the syrup reaches 300°F on a candy thermometer. (Don't let the candy thermometer touch the bottom of the hot pan or you won't get an accurate reading.) Add the almonds and stir to coat with the sugar syrup. Pour the mixture onto the prepared cookie sheet. Use the lemon half to press the almonds into an even layer. Work quickly and be careful—they're very hot! When cool, break them into small pieces and serve.

This brittle is simple to make and great for that holiday cookie swap. We guarantee you'll make a lot of new friends with it.

>>>> *Shared at the table with...* <<<<

_____

_____

_____

_____

If you really want to make a friend, go to someone's house and eat with him...the people who give you their food give you their heart.

—*Cesar Chavez*

Panettone Ricotta Bombe

MAKES 12 SERVINGS

Panettone is a sweet Italian bread that originated in Milan. It typically contains candied orange, citron, raisins, and lemon zest, or it may be plain or studded with chocolate chips. It's an Italian tradition to give panettone as a gift during the Christmas and New Year season. Around the holidays, you can easily find premade and boxed versions, and that is what is called for in this show-stopping dessert.

The panettone ricotta bombe is very festive looking and decadently delicious as a dessert or for a holiday brunch. We use homemade limoncello to make this dish, but you can substitute Grand Marnier, Chambord, or your favorite liqueur. Serve the bombe with a glass of champagne.

>>> *Shared at the table with…* <<<

_____

_____

_____

_____

_____

¼ cup sugar

¼ cup limoncello

1 small (17.5 oz./500g) panettone

1 recipe Sweet Ricotta Cream Filling (see page 70)

Confectioners' sugar, for serving (optional)

First, make the limoncello simple syrup. In a small saucepan bring ½ cup water, the sugar, and limoncello to a boil over medium heat, stirring until the sugar has dissolved. Set aside to cool.

Next, assemble the bombe. Line a 9-inch-wide, 5-inch-deep bowl with plastic wrap and set aside. Cut a ½-inch-thick slice off the top of and a ½-inch-thick slice off the bottom of the panettone and set them aside. Cut the rest of the panettone in half vertically. Now cut each half into ½-inch slices.

Place the top slice of the panettone in the bottom of the bowl cut side up. Drizzle 1 tablespoon of the limoncello syrup over it. Quickly dip one side of all of the ½-inch slices in the syrup. Stand dipped slices all around the bowl, dipped side facing inward. Spread ½ cup of the sweet ricotta cream filling over the bottom slice in the bowl. Layer a few more slices of panettone over the ricotta. Add another layer of ricotta cream. Continue layering panettone slices and ricotta. Finish the layering with ½ cup ricotta and the bottom slice of panettone—cut side down. Cover with a round piece of parchment paper, and then cover with plastic wrap. Refrigerate 12 hours or overnight.

To serve, uncover and remove parchment. Invert the bombe onto a cake plate and remove plastic wrap. Sprinkle with confectioners' sugar before serving.

PART THREE

SPRING

Asparagus Crostata

MAKES 8 SERVINGS

Crostata *is the Italian word for "tart." Thanks to the prolific asparagus patch in the garden, we've found this dish to be very versatile. Cut into small squares it's a fine appetizer, but more generous portions can be served as a breakfast, as a light lunch, or as dinner with a soup course and a salad.*

—————————————

→→→→ *Shared at the* ←←←←
table with...

_____

_____

_____

For a photograph of this dish, turn the page

¼ recipe Pie Crust (see page 118)

2 tablespoons butter

1 tablespoon olive oil

1 small onion, chopped (about ½ cup)

1 garlic clove, chopped

½ pound asparagus spears, trimmed and sliced ¼ inch thick, plus 8 asparagus spears, trimmed

½ teaspoon salt

¼ teaspoon black pepper (about 12 turns on a grinder)

3 large eggs

½ cup heavy cream

¼ cup grated Pecorino Romano cheese

1 teaspoon fresh thyme leaves

2 tablespoons Italian-style breadcrumbs

½ cup chopped sliced provolone cheese

¼ cup garlic-herb cheese (such as Boursin or a chèvre from your local farmers' market)

1 egg (optional)

2 tablespoons cream (optional)

—————————————

Preheat oven to 375°F. On a lightly floured work surface roll out the dough to a 12-inch round (or other shape). Lift the dough and fit into a 9-inch tart pan with a removable bottom, pressing the dough into the pan and forming a high edge. Refrigerate while you prepare the filling.

In a large skillet, melt the butter with the oil over medium heat. Add onion and garlic and cook, stirring occasionally until they begin to soften—about 5 minutes. Add the ½ pound sliced asparagus, salt, and pepper. Cook, stirring occasionally, until tender—5 to 7 minutes. Set aside to cool.

In a small bowl, mix eggs, cream, Pecorino Romano, and thyme. Sprinkle the crust with 1 tablespoon of breadcrumbs. Spread the cooled asparagus mixture over the crust. Add provolone and dot with garlic-herb cheese.

Pour cream and egg mixture over the asparagus. Sprinkle the remaining breadcrumbs on top. Arrange the asparagus spears on top and push them into the custard a bit.

Here we've added an optional decorative touch with leaves carved from the leftover dough scraps which have been cut into a rectangle. If you'd like to add extra sheen to the crust, make an egg wash by beating 1 egg with 2 tablespoons of cream and brushing over the dough.

Bake on the lowest shelf of your oven for about 40 minutes or until the crostata is golden and puffy.

Note: You can use whatever cheese you have in the refrigerator such as mozzarella, Gruyère, provolone, or Parmigiano.

Asparagus Crostata (page 134)

Crostini with Artichoke and Pea Pestos

MAKES 24 APPETIZERS

In the late spring and early summer, we can make a meal out of a bottle of rosé and these little crunchy breads topped with unusual pestos. The flavors of the cheeses with fresh herbs and the crostini combine to make your palate beg for more. The pestos here can also be used as sauce for hot or cold pasta dishes or as a sandwich spread. The best time to make this dish is in early summer when the peas from the garden are young, sweet, and small. If you don't plant peas, shop at a local farmers' market or produce store and ask for the young peas. If using fresh peas, you'll need to blanch them first. If all else fails, the supermarket bags of baby sweet peas will do just fine.

→→→ *Shared at the table with…* ←←←

_____

_____

_____

_____

2 loaves Italian bread or French baguettes, sliced ½ inch thick

Olive oil

1 large garlic clove, peeled and halved lengthwise

1 recipe Pea Pesto (below)

1 recipe Artichoke Pesto (below)

Sun-dried tomato strips, for garnish

Fresh herbs, for garnish

Move an oven rack to the middle position and preheat oven to 400°F. Brush both sides of the bread slices with oil and place on a cookie sheet. Bake crostini about 5 minutes or until golden. Rub both sides of each slice of toasted bread with the cut side of the garlic. Spread each piece of bread with artichoke pesto or pea pesto. Garnish pea pesto crostini with sun-dried tomato strips. Garnish artichoke crostini with fresh herbs.

ARTICHOKE PESTO

One 14-ounce can artichokes hearts packed in water

2 large garlic cloves

½ cup walnuts

Zest and juice from 1 large lemon

½ cup olive oil

½ cup fresh parsley

½ cup fresh basil leaves

¼ cup fresh mint leaves

⅔ cup grated aged goat cheese (you can substitute grated Parmigiano or Grana Padano cheese)

Salt and pepper

Drain artichokes; rinse well. Place the garlic, walnuts, lemon juice, and oil in a food processor. Pulse a few times to chop the garlic and walnuts. Add the parsley, basil, and mint

and pulse a few times until the herbs are finely chopped. Add the artichokes and pulse until the artichokes are still chunky. Add the lemon zest, cheese, and salt and pepper to taste; pulse to combine. Transfer to a bowl.

PEA PESTO

2 cups shelled fresh peas (frozen peas may also be used)

1 scallion, sliced

1 garlic clove

1/4 cup pine nuts (you can substitute walnuts)

Juice of 1 lemon

A few fresh mint leaves

1 teaspoon salt

1/4 teaspoon black pepper

1/2 cup olive oil

1/2 cup grated Parmigiano cheese

Rinse peas in a colander and drain well. Place peas, scallion, garlic, nuts, lemon juice, mint, and salt and pepper in a food processor and pulse to chop. While the machine is running, gradually pour in the oil until the pesto is well blended and smooth. Add the cheese and pulse to combine. Taste and add more salt if necessary. Transfer to a bowl.

Field Greens, Fig, and Brie Salad

MAKES 8 SERVINGS

12 fresh figs

8 cups mixed field greens

8 ounces Brie, cubed

1 tangerine, juiced

3 tablespoons white balsamic vinegar

¼ cup extra-virgin olive oil

Salt and pepper

Wash and drain figs. Remove stems and halve figs lengthwise. In a large salad bowl, toss the greens with the figs and Brie. In a small bowl, whisk together tangerine juice, vinegar, oil, and salt and pepper to taste. Pour over the salad; toss to coat.

One (of the many) valuable lesson we've learned from our transition from city dwellers to country folk is that simple is the new luxury. Never has this truth been more tastefully presented than in this easy and elegant salad.

>>>> *Shared at the table with...* <<<<

_____

_____

_____

_____

Wishing to be friends is quick work, but friendship is a slow-ripening fruit.

—*Aristotle*

Nonna's Bread Soup

MAKES 4 SERVINGS

You can make great meals out of simple ingredients. Nothing better proves this concept than bread soup. The soup is a simple combination of water, egg, and some leftover hard bread that most folks would throw away; the results are delicious.

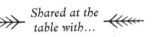
Shared at the table with...

2 tablespoons olive oil

1 large garlic clove, thinly sliced

2 chicken bouillon cubes

2 tablespoons chopped fresh parsley

2 slices Italian bread, cut into 1-inch cubes (about 2 cups)

2 plum tomatoes, diced

2 mushrooms, sliced

2 large eggs, beaten

2 tablespoons grated Pecorino Romano cheese

In a medium saucepan, heat oil over medium-low heat; fry the garlic until lightly golden—about 1 minute. Be careful not to let the garlic burn as this will cause a bitter taste. Add 4 cups of water, the bouillon, parsley, bread, tomatoes, and mushrooms.

Bring soup to a simmer and cook 5 minutes until bread softens. While stirring the soup, pour the eggs into the hot soup to create ribbons of egg.

Ladle into soup bowls and sprinkle with cheese.

Note: If you want to add some protein to make this a heartier offering, you may add 4 unbeaten eggs to the soup and poach them for 3 minutes in the hot stock. Float one poached egg atop each bowl served.

Note

You can replace the water and bouillon cubes with 4 cups of chicken stock.

Maria's Vegetable Minestrone

MAKES 8 SERVINGS

Up until the 1960s in Sicily and the 1940s in America, meat was scarce and expensive. Times were tough in Sicily during and after WWII, and most families ate mainly vegetables. Rose Marie's family lived in a rural area and her papa was able to forage for wild vegetables and herbs. That's when little Rose Marie first started perfecting this minestrone.

→→→ *Shared at the table with...* ←←←

¼ cup olive oil

2 celery stalks, sliced

1 large onion, diced

¼ cup chopped fresh parsley

6 plum tomatoes, diced

Salt and pepper

2 large potatoes, peeled and diced

1 bunch kale, chopped

1 pound ditalini or other small shell pasta

1 cup frozen baby peas, rinsed

One 15.5-ounce can cannellini beans, drained and rinsed

One 15.5-ounce can kidney beans, drained and rinsed

Grated Pecorino Romano cheese, for serving

Extra-virgin olive oil, for serving

In a small saucepan, heat oil over medium heat. Add celery, onion, and parsley. Cook, stirring occasionally, until onion is golden brown—about 5 minutes. Add tomatoes, season with salt and pepper to taste, and cook until lightly thickened—5 minutes. Set aside.

In a large pot, bring 5 quarts of water to a boil over medium-high heat. Add the potatoes, kale, pasta, and salt to taste. Simmer 8 minutes or until pasta is al dente. Drain half of the water. The remaining mixture should be soupy. Add reserved celery-onion-tomato mixture, peas, and both types of beans to the pasta. Simmer to combine all ingredients. Continue to cook for a few minutes so that the flavors can blend. Taste and correct for salt if, necessary.

Serve in large bowls with grated Romano cheese and a drizzle of olive oil.

Doreen's Scones

MAKES 12 SCONES

2 cups all-purpose flour

⅓ cup sugar

1 tablespoon baking powder

5 tablespoons cold butter

¾ cup milk

⅓ cup dried cherries

Finely grated zest from 1 small orange

Flour for shaping the scones

Move a rack to the middle position in the oven and preheat oven to 450°F.

Combine the flour, sugar, and baking powder; stir well with a fork. Using the large holes of a box grater, grate butter into the flour; use your fingers to toss the butter into the flour and coat it well. Alternatively, you can pulse the butter and flour together in a food processor until the butter is cut into pea-sized chunks. Add the milk to the butter and flour mixture and mix until just combined. Stir in the cherries and zest.

Gather the dough and shape into a circle, pressing so the dough comes together.

Place the dough on a lightly floured work surface and fold dough over itself a few times until it holds together. Shape into a 12-inch square about ½ inch thick. Cut the dough into 12 equal triangles and place on a baking sheet, spacing them 1 inch apart. Bake 12 minutes or until golden brown.

To be a good neighbor, you need a staple "come a-calling" recipe. A good neighbor like Rose Marie's friend Doreen will never show up empty handed. These scones are perfect right out of the oven and can last for several days when kept in an airtight container. For a variation, use lemon zest instead of the orange and substitute ⅓ cup raisins for the cherries.

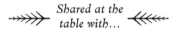

Shared at the table with...

Caramelized Onion–Walnut Focaccia

MAKES 12 SERVINGS

We did a variation of this easy recipe in our very first cookbook, The Beekman 1802 Heirloom Cookbook. *It has become a modern classic. Here we've done a few little flavor twists that highlight how versatile the original recipe is.*

→→→ *Shared at the table with…* ←←←

What if you gave someone a gift, and they neglected to thank you for it—would you be likely to give them another? Life is the same way. In order to attract more of the blessings that life has to offer, you must truly appreciate what you already have.

— Ralph Marston

2 tablespoons olive oil

1 large Vidalia onion, halved and thinly sliced

Salt and pepper

Olive oil spray

1 pound Breakfast of Champions Pizza dough (page 208) or store-bought pizza dough

1 teaspoon each of chopped fresh rosemary, parsley, and thyme

1 tablespoon Parmigiano cheese

1 cup goat cheese crumbles

¼ cup chopped walnuts

1 rosemary sprig for garnish (optional)

In a large skillet, heat oil over medium heat. Add the onion and cook, stirring occasionally, until it's a golden-brown color—20 to 30 minutes. Add a bit more oil if necessary to continue browning. Season with salt and pepper to taste and set aside.

Move an oven rack to the lowest position and preheat the oven to 400°F. Spray a 10- by 14-inch rimmed baking pan with olive oil spray. Place the dough in the pan and use your fingers to push and stretch the dough evenly into the pan. Sprinkle rosemary, parsley, and thyme evenly over the dough. Cover with a cotton dish towel, making sure the towel does not touch the dough, and let rise for 30 minutes.

Cover dough with the cooked onions, Parmigiano, goat cheese, walnuts, and rosemary sprig. Bake 20 to 30 minutes until crust is golden brown. Start checking the focaccia after 20 minutes.

Cool 5 minutes, and then lift focaccia out of the pan and place on a cutting board. Cut into 12 squares. Can be served warm or at room temperature.

GOAT
CHEESE

FOCACCIA

CARAMELIZED
ONIONS

HONEY

WALNUTS

Bon Appétit

ROSEMARY

Ramp Butter

MAKES 2 LOGS, 8 TABLESPOONS EACH

Ramps are wild leeks that have tulip-like green leaves, a scallion-like stalk, and a small bulb; the end of April or beginning of May is ramp season in Sharon Springs. For the most part, the cold and snow of winter is gone, and many of our neighbors in the area head into the woods to forage for the first wild edibles of the season—ramps. Many families even have their own secret patch and closely guard its location. If you don't have a secret ramp patch of your own, you can likely buy ramps at the farmers' markets. You can also use this same process to make other flavored butters from early-season greens such as garlic scapes or chives.

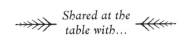

Shared at the
table with…

1 bunch (4 ounces)
ramps, cleaned

16 tablespoons unsalted
butter, cut into cubes

1 teaspoon kosher salt

In a medium pot of boiling water cook the ramps 30 seconds to blanch, then dunk into an ice water bath to halt cooking; drain. In a food processor, pulse the ramps, butter, and salt until well combined. Divide in half, wrap each half in plastic wrap, shape each half into a log, and freeze.

Sautéed Baby Peas

MAKES 4 SERVINGS

2 tablespoons butter

2 tablespoons olive oil

1 small onion, finely chopped

2 tablespoons chopped prosciutto

1 package (10 ounces) frozen baby peas, thawed (use fresh if you have them available)

½ teaspoon sugar

Salt and pepper

In a medium saucepan, heat butter and oil over medium heat. Add the onion and cook, stirring occasionally until golden—5 minutes. Add prosciutto and cook for 1 minute. Add peas, sugar, and salt and pepper to taste. Cover and cook until piping hot and the flavors have come together—about 10 minutes.

Note: These peas pair beautifully with Chicken on a Stick (page 173).

It was growing sweet peas and shelling them for dinner that made us appreciate all of the farm labor that goes into harvesting and preparing the foods that grace tables all across America every single day. You have to shell a lot of peas to get 2 cups ready for cooking, and if you didn't do that part of the work, someone else did.

This recipe is for all of those people who labor for us in ways that we might never fully comprehend.

When you have more than you need, build a bigger table, not a higher fence. Invite as many as possible to have a seat.

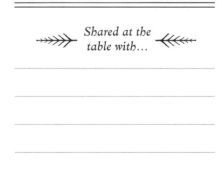

Shared at the table with…

_____

_____

_____

_____

Braised Artichokes

MAKES 4 SERVINGS

People are often afraid of cooking artichokes, but this recipe makes it simple. These artichokes can be served as an appetizer or a side dish. For a slightly different take, add some cured meat such as chopped salami or mortadella into the breadcrumb mixture.

=====

→→→ *Shared at the table with...* ←←←

_____

_____

_____

_____

4 medium artichokes

½ lemon

½ cup Italian-style breadcrumbs

1 large garlic clove, finely chopped

2 tablespoons chopped fresh parsley

½ cup grated Pecorino Romano cheese

½ teaspoon kosher salt

½ teaspoon pepper

½ cup olive oil

1 large egg

Clean and trim artichokes by snapping off dark green tough outer leaves until only pale green tender leaves remain. Cut off the top third of each artichoke. Use a vegetable peeler to peel the stems. Rub with lemon as you're trimming to prevent browning. Gently pry open the leaves at the top of each artichoke, and use a long spoon to scrape and remove the hairy choke from the center. Place the cleaned artichokes in a bowl of water with the rest of the lemon while you prepare the bread filling.

In a medium bowl, combine the breadcrumbs, garlic, parsley, cheese, salt, pepper, and ¼ cup of the oil. Mix well. Drain the artichokes, and use your fingers to spread the leaves apart. Sprinkle breadcrumb mixture in between the leaves. With your hand, pat the leaves down over the leaves to make sure the breadcrumbs are in place.

Beat the egg until smooth and drizzle the top of each artichoke with the egg. In a pot large enough to hold the artichokes in a single layer, heat the remaining oil over medium heat. Fry the artichokes with their stems facing up until golden to create a seal on the top of the artichokes. Turn them on their sides and continue to cook until browned on all sides. Add 1 cup of water to the pot and bring to a simmer. Lower the heat and place a wet cotton

dish towel over the pot. Cover and bring the corners of
the dish towel over the lid to prevent the cloth from burn-
ing on the burner. Simmer on low for 30 minutes. Turn
the artichokes after 15 minutes and add more water if
necessary. Cover and continue to cook another 15 minutes, checking periodically to be sure the artichokes don't
scorch. Check for tenderness by inserting a sharp knife
into the base of an artichoke. The blade should slide in
easily with very little resistance. There will be almost no
liquid left in the pot when the chokes are finished cooking.
Serve warm.

Eat by peeling off each leaf and biting off the broad end.
Save the meaty artichoke "heart" (the bottom center of the
vegetable) for the delicious last bites.

Stuffed Onions

We've stuffed mushrooms, bell peppers, potatoes, and zucchini blossoms (see page 198), so it only seemed natural to give stuffed onions a try. Served as an entrée, these make for a light but satisfying meal.

>>>>> *Shared at the table with...* <<<<<

---

4 large white onions (we prefer a sweet onion like Vidalia, but use your favorite)

¼ cup olive oil

3 garlic cloves, chopped

1 red bell pepper, seeded and coarsely chopped

½ pound Italian fennel sausage, casings removed

½ pound 93% lean ground beef

2 large eggs

1 teaspoon dried oregano

2 tablespoons chopped fresh parsley

Salt and pepper

½ cup grated Parmigiano cheese, plus more for serving

½ cup Italian-style breadcrumbs

1 cup beef stock

Move an oven rack to the lowest position and preheat the oven to 375°F.

Trim about ½-inch from the onion tops and just enough from the bottoms so they can stand upright. With an ice cream scoop or a spoon, scoop out the layers of onion, leaving about a ½-inch thick wall. Finely chop the scooped-out onion layers.

In a large skillet, heat the oil over medium-high heat. Add the chopped onion, garlic, and red pepper; cook, stirring occasionally, until the vegetables are tender—about 5 minutes. Add the sausage and ground meat and cook, stirring to break up lumps until browned. Remove from the heat.

In a large bowl, whisk together the eggs, oregano, parsley, and salt and pepper to taste. Add the cooked meat, cheese, and breadcrumbs, and mix well. Spoon meat mixture into the onion shells and place the onions in a baking dish.

Pour stock around the onions. Cover with foil and bake
30 minutes. Uncover and bake 20 minutes more or until
the onions are tender when pierced with a knife. Let
stand for a couple of minutes before serving. Sprinkle with
additional Parmigiano cheese and serve.

Homemade Ricotta

MAKES 4 CUPS

While you can find very good Italian cheeses, including ricotta, in specialty delis or cheese shops, it's not nearly as good as what you can make at home. Get the kids involved; homemade ricotta is an excellent activity for children. To make ricotta at home, you'll need a large colander and a piece of fine-mesh cheesecloth. The liquid that drips from the ricotta is called whey; save the whey to cook risotto and pasta, using it instead of water. You might also want to try the My Whey Cocktail.

1 gallon whole milk

2 cups heavy cream

1 teaspoon fine sea salt

7 tablespoons fresh lemon juice

2 tablespoons champagne vinegar (can substitute white wine vinegar)

Line a large colander with a double layer of fine-mesh cheesecloth and place the lined colander over a large bowl.

In a large heavy saucepan or enameled pot, slowly bring milk, cream, and salt to a rolling boil (one that you can't stir down), stirring occasionally to prevent scorching. Add lemon juice and vinegar, and then reduce heat to low and simmer, stirring constantly, until the mixture curdles—about 2 minutes.

MY WHEY COCKTAIL

Whey can serve as a great digestif—an after-dinner drink that aids in the digestion of the meal you've just consumed. This delicious cocktail can also serve as a replacement for a full dessert.

To make the My Whey Cocktail, simply mix 4 ounces of cold whey or milk with a shot of coffee liqueur. Serve over ice with shaved chocolate.

Ladle the curds into the lined colander and let the cheese drain for 1 hour. Transfer the drained ricotta to a container; cover and refrigerate. The ricotta will keep in the refrigerator for several days.

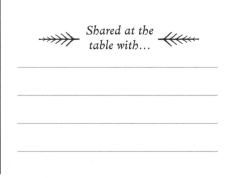

Shared at the table with…

_____

_____

_____

_____

Spaghetti Frittata

6 large eggs

5 cups cooked spaghetti

¼ cup grated Pecorino Romano cheese

¼ cup grated Parmigiano cheese

2 tablespoon chopped fresh parsley

½ teaspoon salt

¼ teaspoon black pepper

⅛ teaspoon red pepper flakes

½ cup milk

3 tablespoons olive oil

Extra grated cheese and parsley for garnish

Frugality can be turned into a culinary art form. Combining eggs with leftover spaghetti may not seem like a tasty way to start the day, but trust us, no one who's sat down at our table on a Sunday morning has ever complained.

>>>⟫ *Shared at the table with...* ⟪<<<

In a large bowl beat the eggs with a fork. Add the spaghetti, both cheeses, parsley, salt, black pepper, red pepper, and milk. Mix well.

In a large nonstick skillet, heat oil over medium heat. Pour spaghetti mixture into the pan. Cover and cook 10 minutes. The frittata will set and get puffy, and the bottom should be golden. Use water to wet a plate that is larger than the skillet. Cover the frittata with the plate, and then flip the frittata over onto the plate. (Do this over the sink. You may have some egg drippings.) Slide the frittata back into the pan and continue to cook until it's golden on the bottom. Slide the frittata onto a serving plate. Cut into wedges and serve. Garnish with cheese and parsley.

Raviolo Filled with Egg Yolk

FILLING MAKES 6 RAVIOLI

This dish is perfect for a small dinner party, especially if you want to dazzle your guests. For best results, buy your eggs from a farmer or farmers' market that sells fresh organic eggs. While you'll pay a little more, the difference the fresh yolk makes in this recipe is well worth the cost.

In this recipe, you basically serve one large raviolo per guest.

This recipe makes more dough than you need for the six ravioli. You can roll the extra into fettucine for another meal, or make and freeze extra squares. To freeze, place the pasta squares between sheets of plastic wrap and wrap in foil. The squares may turn darker once they're frozen, which is just fine. You can use these squares to make ravioli, lasagna, or manicotti.

⟶⟶⟶ *Shared at the table with...* ⟵⟵⟵

PASTA DOUGH

1 cup all-purpose flour

½ cup 00 flour (you can substitute all-purpose flour)

2 large eggs

1 tablespoon white wine

2 teaspoons milk

Flour for rolling out pasta

Flour for baking sheet

FILLING

1½ cups ricotta

1 tablespoon finely chopped fresh parsley

¼ cup grated

Parmigiano cheese

¼ cup grated Pecorino Romano cheese

⅛ teaspoon nutmeg

¼ teaspoon kosher salt plus 2 tablespoons for the pasta cooking water

⅛ teaspoon white pepper

6 small fresh eggs

Kosher salt

SAGE–BROWN BUTTER SAUCE

1 stick butter

12 sage leaves, 6 whole and 6 thinly cut into ribbons

First, make the pasta. Place the flours in the bowl of a food processor. In a measuring cup with a spout, lightly beat the eggs, wine, and milk together. With the processor running, gradually pour the egg mixture through the feed tube into the flours. Process until dough comes together. Pinch a small amount of dough between your thumb and forefinger. It should stick and feel smooth. You may need to add a few tablespoons of water or flour to get the right consistency. If the dough feels dry and is not holding together, add 1 tablespoon of water at a time until you get a more pliant consistency. If the dough is too sticky, sprinkle in flour and knead until it is no longer tacky. Dust your work surface with additional flour. Then knead using the heel of your hand, turning the dough over and then turning it again.

Continued

Raviolo Filled with Egg Yolk

CONTINUED

Knead until the dough is smooth—about 10 minutes. Place dough in a plastic bag and let it rest for 30 minutes.

Remove the dough from the bag and cut the dough into four equal pieces. Working with one piece at a time and keeping the others covered with a clean dish towel, lightly dust with flour and use your fingers to press the piece into a thin square.

If you're using a pasta machine, set the machine to its widest setting and feed the dough through the rollers. Dust the extruded dough with flour, fold in half and feed another time through the pasta machine at its widest setting. Reshape the edges of the dough to keep them squared. Roll the dough again, lowering the settings incrementally until you have a $1/16$-inch-thick, long sheet of dough.

If you are not using a machine, divide the dough into eight portions instead of four to make rolling it by hand easier. On a floured surface large enough for cutting 4-inch squares, roll the dough to $1/16$-inch thickness. (One of our special tricks is to roll the dough sandwiched between two Silpat sheets, which reduces the amount of flour needed and helps keep the dough from becoming too tough.)

Cut the pasta sheets into squares—about 4 inches, and set the squares on lightly floured sheet pans; cover with plastic wrap. Set the pasta scraps on another sheet pan to use as maltagliati (which basically means "badly cut") pasta in soups.

Sprinkle a baking sheet with flour and set aside.

Now make the filling. In a small bowl, mix together the ricotta, parsley, both cheeses, the nutmeg, salt, and white pepper until well blended.

Spoon ¼ cup of filling into the center of a square of pasta dough and make a well in the ricotta by pressing with an egg in its shell. Build up the walls of the ricotta well. Break eggs one at a time over a bowl, use your hand to separate the yolk from the white, and gently place the egg yolk in the ricotta well. Brush the edges of dough with egg white. Gently cover the pasta square and filling with another square of pasta dough; start at one side of the pasta square and drape the pasta square over the filling and egg to the opposite side. Press edges together with your fingers, making sure to push out any air pockets.

Use your thumb to seal and push air out as you go around the edge of the ricotta. Cut the edges of the raviolo with a fluted pastry wheel to seal.

Once formed, gently lift each raviolo with your hand and set aside on the prepared sheet pan.

Bring a large pot of water to a boil and add 2 tablespoons kosher salt to the water.

While you're waiting for the water to boil, prepare the sage–brown butter sauce. In a large skillet, melt the butter over medium-high heat and cook until golden brown. Add the whole sage and cook a few seconds until crisp; set fried sage aside.

Use a flat spatula to gently transfer each raviolo into the water. Cook 3 minutes. The yolk will be runny after 3 minutes, so you may cook the ravioli a bit longer to your liking. Cook only three ravioli at a time so that you don't overcrowd the pot. After the ravioli are finished cooking, use a slotted spoon to lift out each ravioli and place in the skillet with the browned butter and sage ribbons. Sauté for about 1 minute. Spoon butter sauce over the ravioli. Plate in a heated pasta bowl. Drizzle with the sage butter. Garnish with fried sage leaves and grated Parmigiano.

Orecchiette Pasta with Sausage and Broccoli Rabe

MAKES 4 SERVINGS

Broccoli rabe is slightly pungent, which imparts a delicious flavor when combined with the sweetness of sausage and sautéed garlic. If you don't care for broccoli rabe, you can substitute broccoli.

>>>>> *Shared at the table with...* <<<<<

2 tablespoons olive oil

2 links sweet Italian sausage, casings removed

1 small onion, finely chopped

4 garlic cloves, crushed

¼ teaspoon red pepper flakes

¼ cup white wine

6 sun-dried tomatoes, packed in oil, thinly sliced

1 bunch broccoli rabe, cut into 1-inch pieces, washed and drained

1 chicken bouillon cube

2 tablespoons butter

Salt

½ pound orecchiette pasta (you can substitute any small pasta shells)

Grated Pecorino Romano cheese and red pepper flakes to serve at the table

In a large skillet, heat the oil over medium heat. Add the sausage, onion, garlic, and red pepper. Cook, stirring to break up any lumps, until the sausage is browned. Add the wine, tomatoes, and broccoli rabe; stir until wilted. Add the bouillon cube and 1 cup of water (or replace both with 1 cup of chicken stock), then the butter and simmer until the broccoli rabe is tender. Check for salt and adjust if necessary.

Meanwhile, in a large pot of boiling salted water, cook the pasta until al dente. Drain out most of the water and add the broccoli rabe mixture. Mix and serve topped with the cheese and additional pepper.

Mushroom Risotto

8 cups vegetable stock

1 small piece of Parmigiano cheese rind

3 tablespoons olive oil

10 ounces sliced baby bella mushrooms (about 2½ cups)

½ cup finely chopped onion

1 garlic clove, finely chopped

2 cups arborio rice

½ cup dry white wine

Salt and pepper

3 tablespoons finely chopped fresh parsley

2 tablespoons butter

½ cup grated Parmigiano Reggiano

1 teaspoon truffle oil

This vegetarian dish is perfect for large gatherings by simply doubling or tripling the recipe. The mushroom flavor is earthy but not overpowering, and the dish is hearty enough to serve alone as a meal.

→→→→ *Shared at the table with...* ←←←←

_____

_____

_____

_____

In a medium saucepan, warm the stock with the cheese rind over low heat.

In a large skillet, heat 2 tablespoons of the oil over medium-high heat. Add the mushrooms and cook until tender—3 minutes. Set aside.

In a large saucepan, heat the remaining 1 tablespoon of oil over medium-low heat; stir in the onion and garlic. Cook, stirring occasionally, until the onion is translucent—5 minutes. Add the rice, stirring until coated; cook until the rice is pale gold and translucent—2 minutes. Pour in the wine, stirring constantly, until fully absorbed—2 minutes.

Add ½ cup of warmed stock to the rice, and stir until the stock is absorbed. Continue adding stock, ½ cup at a time, stirring continuously, until the liquid is absorbed and the rice is al dente—18 to 20 minutes. (You might have leftover stock.) Add salt and pepper to taste. Stir in the prepared mushrooms, parsley, butter, grated cheese, and truffle oil.

Rose Marie's Pork Chops

MAKES 6 SERVINGS

When we decided to partner with Rose Marie for this cookbook, we knew this recipe had to be included. This dish is the first recipe Rose Marie ever had published; it appeared in the Westchester Journal News *in March 1993.*

→→→ *Shared at the table with...* ←←←

_____

_____

_____

_____

Six 1-inch-thick boneless pork chops (1½ pounds)

Salt and pepper

2 garlic cloves, minced

2 tablespoons olive oil

1 medium onion, coarsely chopped

½ cup white wine

¼ cup balsamic vinegar

3 slices Genoa salami, diced

12 pitted black cured olives

1 tablespoon pine nuts

½ cup beef stock

With a sharp knife, score the meat lightly on both sides and rub with salt and pepper to taste, and garlic. In a skillet large enough to hold the chops in a single layer, heat the oil over medium heat. Add the chops and cook until browned on both sides. Remove and set aside.

Add the onion to the pan and cook, stirring occasionally until golden brown—7 minutes.

Raise the heat to high. Stir in the wine and vinegar and cook until the liquid is almost evaporated. Add the salami, olives, pine nuts, stock, and ½ cup water; return the pork chops to the pan. Spoon some of the sauce over the top of the chops and cover. Lower the heat and simmer the chops until cooked through—40 to 45 minutes.

Pour the pan juices over the chops before serving.

Beef Braciole with Sunday Tomato Sauce

MAKES 8 SERVINGS

Dinners at Rose Marie's home are traditional Italian. There are multiple courses and the meals can pleasantly go on for hours, especially on Sundays when a pot of tomato sauce (referred to as "gravy") simmers on the stovetop all day. Some of the best conversations are had while everyone's appetite cooks up. The Sunday sauce often becomes the basis for meals throughout the rest of the week, fortified with goodies like sausages and meatballs.

Beef braciole is served as the second course of a Sunday meal or on other special occasions. Traditionally they're cooked alongside sausages and meatballs in a tomato sauce.

You may add browned sausages to the sauce after the braciole have cooked for 20 minutes, and then add fried meatballs to the sauce. Continue cooking over low heat, stirring gently from time to time, until all the meats are cooked. Simmer another 30 minutes or so. Any leftover sauce and meat can be packed in containers and frozen.

SUNDAY TOMATO SAUCE

¼ cup olive oil

1 onion, finely chopped

2 garlic cloves, sliced

One 6-ounce can tomato paste

One 28-ounce can crushed tomatoes

One 28-ounce can petite diced tomatoes

1 bay leaf, preferably fresh

2 whole cloves

Salt and pepper

BRACIOLE

8 large eggs

4 large, thin slices of beef top round (ask for "braciole" meat at the butcher counter)—the larger the better (about 1½ to 2 pounds total)

Salt and pepper

2 garlic cloves, minced

2 tablespoons chopped fresh parsley

½ cup Italian-style breadcrumbs

12 thin slices Genoa salami

¼ cup shaved Parmigiano cheese

1 small onion, halved and thinly sliced

½ cup raisins

¼ cup pine nuts

¼ cup grated Pecorino Romano cheese

2 medium russet potatoes, peeled and thinly sliced

Olive oil for frying

First make the Sunday tomato sauce. In a 5-quart stainless steel saucepan, heat the oil over medium heat. Add the onion and garlic and cook, stirring occasionally, until they're a pale golden color. Add the tomato paste and cook for 5 minutes to caramelize the paste, stirring casually. Fill the tomato paste can with water and stir to dissolve any paste left in the can, then add the water to the pot. Add another canful of water to the pot. Stir to dissolve the paste fully. Add the crushed tomatoes to the pot; fill the can

Continued

Note

Leftover tomato sauce is great for poaching eggs (page 106).

Beef Braciole with Sunday Tomato Sauce

CONTINUED

Shared at the table with…

with water and stir to release any tomatoes left in the can; then add the water do the pot. Do the same with the diced tomatoes—adding the tomatoes, then filling the can with water and adding the water to the pot. Add the bay leaf, cloves, and salt and pepper to taste. Simmer for 1 hour, stirring occasionally. Remove the bay leaf and cloves. (To make the cloves easy to remove, make a small pouch out of a coffee filter; add the cloves and tie closed with kitchen string. When it's time to remove the cloves, simply take out the pouch.)

Meanwhile, as the sauce is simmering, make the braciole. Place the eggs in a large pot and cover with cold water. Bring to a boil over high heat and simmer for 3 minutes. Remove from the heat, cover, and set aside for 10 minutes. Drain, peel, and cut the eggs in half vertically; set aside.

Place the meat on a cutting board. With a meat mallet, pound the meat to flatten and tenderize. Sprinkle the entire surface of the meat with salt, pepper, garlic, parsley, and breadcrumbs. Layer salami, Parmigiano, onion, raisins, and pine nuts on top of the meat. Then sprinkle the Romano cheese over the filling; place eggs (4 halves per slice of meat) and potatoes across each slice of meat. Roll the meat tightly, tucking in the ends; tie with butcher's twine or secure with strong toothpicks.

In a large skillet, heat the oil over medium-high heat and sear the braciole on all sides until browned. Add to the pot of tomato sauce, reduce to a simmer, cover, and cook 1½ hours or until the meat is tender when pierced with a knife. Take the meat out of the sauce and cool for a few minutes. Cut into 1-inch thick rounds and garnish with more tomato sauce.

Chicken on a Stick

Four 6-ounce boneless, skinless chicken breast halves

Salt and pepper

1 garlic clove, minced

1 very small onion, minced

¼ cup minced fresh parsley leaves

¼ cup grated Pecorino Romano cheese

16 thin slices Genoa salami

16 small pieces (¼-inch by 2 inches) good-quality mozzarella or sliced provolone cheese

12 bay leaves

2 large eggs

1 cup Italian-style breadcrumbs

Olive oil for frying

Lemon wedges for garnish

Spiedini *in Italian means "skewers"— basically any food on a wooden stick. This dish is often used for large family gatherings to celebrate a birthday, anniversary, or other special occasion. We made the recipe here with chicken breasts, but you can also use thin cuts of pork or veal. This recipe pairs beautifully with* Sautéed Baby Peas *(page 151).*

>>>> *Shared at the table with…* <<<<

Rinse the chicken breasts and pat dry with paper towels. Put the breasts on a plate and freeze until firm; this step will make slicing them into thin cutlets much easier. Place a frozen chicken breast on a cutting board lined with paper towels. Place your hand flat on the chicken breast and slice the breast into four very thin cutlets. Repeat with the remaining three breasts. Place cutlets on a sheet of plastic wrap and cover with another sheet of plastic wrap. Use a meat mallet and flatten to 3- by 4-inch slices that are ⅛ inch thick. Repeat with all of the cutlets. Line a baking sheet with wax paper. Place the cutlets on the wax paper and sprinkle with salt and pepper to taste.

In a small bowl, stir together the garlic, onion, and parsley. Spread the mixture evenly on the cutlets and sprinkle with grated Pecorino Romano.

Continued

Lay a slice of salami on each piece of meat. Place a piece of mozzarella over each piece of salami. Roll up pieces tightly, starting on the short end of the chicken cutlet and making sure to enclose the filling completely. Thread a chicken roll onto 2 skewers and then thread a bay leaf onto the skewer. Thread three more chicken rolls with a bay leaf in between each piece of meat—the skewers will have four chicken rolls and three bay leaves. Continue with the rest of the chicken rolls.

Preheat the oven to 375°F. Line a baking sheet with foil and place a wire rack on top.

Beat eggs in a shallow dish. Season with salt and pepper to taste. Put breadcrumbs in another shallow dish. Dip each chicken skewer in egg. Use a spoon to pour any remaining egg all over the chicken rolls. Dredge the coated chicken skewers in breadcrumbs, making sure they are well coated and pressing to adhere the breadcrumbs to the chicken.

In a large skillet, pour enough oil to come about ⅛ of an inch up the side of the skillet; heat the oil over medium-high heat.

Fry the chicken skewers over medium heat, turning them as they turn golden—about 3 minutes per side. Transfer chicken to the baking sheet and bake 10 to 15 minutes, until the chicken is cooked through.

Serve with lemon wedges.

Pan-seared Swordfish with Ginger, Soy, and Chives

MAKES 4 SERVINGS

You'll never find a recipe in any of our cookbooks that's too difficult. Although we like to cook, we don't want to spend our lives cooking . . . there are too many other things to see and do!

>>>>> *Shared at the table with...* <<<<<

The world has enough beautiful mountains and meadows, spectacular skies and serene lakes. It has enough lush forests, flowered fields, and sandy beaches. It has plenty of stars and the promise of a new sunrise and sunset every day. What the world needs more of is people to appreciate and enjoy it.

—Michael Josephson

2 tablespoons dark sesame oil

2 tablespoons rice vinegar

1 tablespoon soy sauce

1 teaspoon minced garlic

1 teaspoon minced fresh ginger

1 tablespoon finely chopped crystallized ginger

1 tablespoon finely chopped red bell pepper

1 tablespoon chopped chives

Four 6-ounce swordfish steaks

Salt and pepper

1 teaspoon vegetable oil

In a small saucepan, cook the sesame oil, vinegar, soy sauce, garlic, fresh ginger, crystallized ginger, red pepper, and chives over low heat until reduced by half. Remove from heat and let cool to room temperature.

Place the fish on a plate and season with salt and pepper to taste.

Heat a cast-iron grill pan over medium heat for 5 minutes. Brush with vegetable oil. Sear the swordfish steaks for 4 to 5 minutes per side, depending on thickness. Midway through cooking each side, rotate each steak a half turn to get nice grill marks. Don't overcook. The centers of the steaks should be dark pink.

To serve, arrange steaks on a platter and spoon the sauce over the steaks.

Note

You can make the sauce
ahead of time and store
it in the refrigerator until
ready to use.

Crab Cakes with Homemade Tartar Sauce

MAKES 4 SERVINGS

CRAB CAKES

½ pound lump crabmeat (may substitute claw meat, or an 8-ounce can of crabmeat)

2 heaping tablespoons mayonnaise

1 teaspoon Dijon mustard

1 tablespoon chopped fresh parsley

1 tablespoon chopped fresh chives

½ teaspoon Old Bay seasoning

⅓ cup Italian-style breadcrumbs

1 large egg

¼ cup panko breadcrumbs

1 tablespoon olive oil

TARTAR SAUCE

½ cup mayonnaise

1 teaspoon fresh lemon juice

3 pitted green olives, finely chopped

3 pitted black olives, finely chopped

1½ teaspoons finely chopped pickled jalapeño pepper

1 teaspoon chopped fresh parsley

Lemon wedges for serving

Brent was only 8 years old when he visited relatives in Baltimore. It was the first time he had tasted Old Bay seasoning, and it was a tastebud–transforming experience. At the time, Old Bay—with its distinctive blend of mustard, paprika, celery salt, bay leaf, black pepper, crushed pepper flakes, mace, cloves, allspice, nutmeg, cardamom, and ginger—was regionally specific, but now chefs and home cooks have made it popular across the country. We've even seen it make its way into cocktails! These crab cakes take advantage of the distinctive Old Bay mix.

>>>> *Shared at the table with…* <<<<

_____

_____

_____

_____

First make the crab cakes. In a large bowl, mix together the crabmeat, mayonnaise, mustard, parsley, chives, Old Bay, Italian-style breadcrumbs, and egg. Shape into 4 patties. Coat the patties with the breadcrumbs, pressing to adhere.

In a large skillet, heat the oil over medium-high heat. Add the patties and cook until golden—3 minutes per side.

To make the tartar sauce, in a medium bowl, stir together the mayonnaise, lemon juice, green and black olives, pickled jalapeño, and parsley.

Serve with the tartar sauce and lemon wedges.

Almond Paste Cookies

MAKES ABOUT 30 COOKIES

Long before we arrived at Beekman Farm, generations of ghost stories had been told about the house—which had been abandoned for a good portion of its recent history. One such ghost is that of a 5-year-old girl, presumably named "Mary" because of a name carved into our hallway floor in a childlike scrawl. A self-proclaimed "ghost whisperer" who visited the house told us that Mary thinks of us as her imaginary friends and often laughs at us as we navigate the trappings of the modern world that now inhabit her house and her imagination. Mary will always have a seat at the table (whether we see her or not).

Almond cookies would have been an exotic luxury during her original time in the house, but we like to think that they would be just perfect for a proper little tea party.

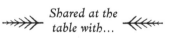

Shared at the table with…

8 ounces almond paste, chilled

⅔ cup sugar

2 large egg whites

1 teaspoon finely grated lemon zest

1 cup sliced almonds

Move an oven rack to the middle position and preheat the oven to 325°F. Line two baking sheets with parchment paper. Using the large holes of a box grater, grate the chilled almond paste and transfer to a large bowl. Add the sugar, egg whites, and lemon zest, and use a hand mixer to beat until smooth. Place the sliced almonds in a small bowl.

Use a teaspoon to scoop dough; roll the scoops in the almonds, pressing to adhere. With your fingers, gently flatten the dough onto the baking sheet, spacing a few inches apart. Bake 20 to 25 minutes, or until the almonds are golden and the cookies are set. Transfer to a wire rack to cool.

Lemon Granita

MAKES 4 SERVINGS

½ cup superfine sugar, possibly more

Lemon zest from 2 lemons cut into strips

½ cup freshly squeezed lemon juice

Fresh mint for garnish

In a small pan, heat 1 cup water and the sugar over medium heat, stirring until the sugar dissolves. Add the lemon zest, remove from heat, cover, and let cool. Add the lemon juice, taste, and correct for sweetness. Transfer to a bowl, cover, and chill. Strain; discard the lemon zest. Pour the liquid into a loaf pan and freeze. Take out of the freezer every 15 minutes and use a fork to scrape the slush from the edges into the center until you have flaky ice crystals. The entire pan will have frozen over the course of 2 hours.

Spoon granita into glasses and serve garnished with mint.

While lemon granita (shaved ice) is a wonderfully cool and soothing dessert on a hot day, it can also be enjoyed on a snowy winter's day. Rose Marie's fondest memory of this dessert is when her mother prepared it on one of the rare occasions when it snowed in Sicily. Basically all that's required on a snowy day is a glass of clean snow, some sugar, and lemon juice.

Here we've provided the more traditional preparation method.

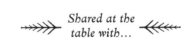

Shared at the table with…

RABBIT GOODY

RABBIT GOODY IS A NATIONAL TREASURE.

She's one of the world's foremost experts on historic textiles. Steven Spielberg has her create all the fabrics for any of his movies that require historic reproductions. She's woven fabric for Chanel, and you can see her handiwork in museums around the world.

For Beekman 1802 she's created everything from scarves to blankets to napkin bibs.

When we first started growing our artisan collective, people commented that we were just lucky that we happened across a community that was so full of talented people. While it's true that we do consider ourselves to be the luckiest of sorts, our response to the notion that we live in a place that is somehow extraordinary is to deny it.

We lived in the same apartment building in NYC for over 10 years. During that time we had dinner with only one neighbor. We've all become so disconnected, so isolated in our own little world, that we seem to have lost interest in what those right next door are doing. Moving to Beekman Farm and meeting people like Rabbit reminded us that there are treasures in every single community. Sometimes all you need to do to discover them is knock on the door.

I am of the opinion that my life belongs to the whole community and as long as I live, it is my privilege to do for it whatever I can. I want to be thoroughly used up when I die, for the harder I work the more I've lived.

—George Bernard Shaw

Ms. Cesa's Cream Cheese Cookies

MAKES ABOUT 60 COOKIES

Did you have that woman in your town who always seemed to have a jar full of cookies? Her age was indeterminate, but she seemed to be a grandmother to generations of neighborhood children? That was Ms. Cesa in Rose Marie's village in Sicily. This is her prized cookie recipe.

→→→ *Shared at the table with...* ←←←

COOKIES

½ cup sugar

2 large eggs

8 ounces cream cheese, room temperature

1 teaspoon vanilla extract

2½ cups all-purpose flour

4 teaspoons baking powder

½ cup salted butter, room temperature

ICING

2¼ cups confectioners' sugar

1 teaspoon each of lemon, orange, and vanilla extract

¼ cup milk

Sprinkles for decorating (optional)

Start by making the cookies. Move a rack to the middle of the oven and preheat the oven to 375°F. Line two baking sheets with parchment. In a large bowl, mix sugar and eggs with a fork. Add cream cheese and vanilla and mix until well combined. In another large bowl, mix flour and baking powder. Use your fingertips to work the butter into the flour until mixture looks like large crumbs.

Add the flour and butter mixture to the egg–cream cheese mixture. Work dough with a fork and then your hands until it is smooth. Shape dough into balls, each about 1 teaspoon, and place 2 inches apart on baking sheets.

Bake 15 minutes or until lightly golden. Transfer cookies to wire racks to cool completely.

Now make the icing. In a small bowl, mix the confectioner's sugar with the extracts and the milk and stir until smooth. Dip tops of cookies into the icing and, if you are using sprinkles, top with sprinkles. Let dry.

Note

You can also only spread the marmalade on one layer, as in the photo, and sandwich the marmalade between the cake layers. Sprinkle with the remaining chopped rosemary.

A Thousand Different Olive Oil Cakes

MAKES 12 TO 16 SERVINGS

2½ cups all-purpose flour

½ teaspoon baking powder

½ teaspoon baking soda

1 teaspoon salt

3 large eggs

2 cups sugar

1 cup extra-virgin olive oil

1 cup milk

2 tablespoons orange liqueur

Zest and juice from 1 orange

2 teaspoons chopped fresh rosemary

½ teaspoon anise seed, crushed

½ teaspoon fennel seed, crushed

6 tablespoons orange marmalade (or whatever you have on hand)

Move an oven rack to the middle positon and preheat oven to 350°F. Grease two 9-inch round cake pans.

In a large bowl, stir together flour, baking powder, baking soda, and salt; set aside.

In another large bowl, beat eggs and sugar with an electric hand-held mixer on low. Add olive oil, milk, liqueur, orange zest, orange juice, 1 teaspoon of the rosemary, the anise seed, and fennel seed; mix on medium speed until blended. Add the flour mixture and mix until well blended.

Divide the batter evenly between the prepared pans. Bake 1 hour, until golden brown and a wooden pick inserted in the center comes out clean. Let cool on wire racks, then run a thin spatula around the sides of the pans and invert onto racks. Turn upright onto cake plates. Spread the cakes with orange marmalade and then stack one on top of the other.

Whenever someone visits Sharon Springs from afar, they always seem to bring with them a jar of their homemade jam. Over the years, we must have tried thousands of different flavor combinations, and we are grateful for the creativity and the love of place poured into each and every one. What we love about this moist cake is that you can use whatever jam or marmalade you happen to have open. Every time you try a new topping you essentially have a whole new cake!

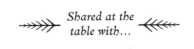

Shared at the table with…

The Essential Biscotti

We were together for 15 years before we tied the knot. Because we already owned way too many things to make wedding gifts necessary, we asked each of the 300 guests to prepare a family heirloom dish for sharing, and to bring the recipe. We set up a 40-foot-long table on the back lawn, and as guests arrived, we took their photos with their recipes and placed their dishes on the table. These crunchy but not-too-sweet biscotti are what Rose Marie shared. There were none left.

3½ cups all-purpose flour, plus extra for dusting

1 teaspoon baking powder

1 teaspoon salt

4 large eggs

2 large egg yolks

2 cups plus 2 tablespoons sugar

2 teaspoons vanilla extract

8 ounces bittersweet chocolate, coarsely chopped

8 ounces white chocolate, coarsely chopped

2 cups almonds, coarsely chopped

2 cups shelled pistachios, coarsely chopped

Flour for work surface

1 large egg white, for glaze

Move oven racks to the lower and middle positions and preheat oven to 325°F. Lightly grease two large cookie sheets or line with parchment.

In a bowl, stir together flour, baking powder, and salt. In a large bowl of an electric mixer on medium speed, beat the eggs, egg yolks, and 2 cups sugar until blended—about 2 minutes. The dough should be pale and thick. Beat in vanilla. Gradually beat in flour mixture until combined.

Fold in the bittersweet chocolate, white chocolate, and nuts. Mix until the dough is well combined.

Flour your work surface and divide dough into 6 equal pieces. Shape each piece of dough into a 1½- by 10-inch log. Use some flour, if necessary, to shape the logs. Place three logs on each baking sheet 3 inches apart. In a small bowl, beat egg white until frothy. With a pastry brush, glaze logs with the beaten egg white and sprinkle with the remaining 2 tablespoons sugar.

Bake the logs for 20 to 25 minutes, until they are lightly golden brown, firm to the touch, and just beginning to crack slightly, rotating the baking sheets from front to back and lower and middle shelves halfway through. Transfer baking sheets to wire racks and let the logs cool completely on the baking sheets.

Reduce oven temperature to 200°F. With a sharp serrated knife, slice the biscotti slightly on a diagonal bias into ¾-inch-thick slices. Lay slices on baking sheets in a single layer. Bake 20 minutes or until firm. Cool the biscotti completely on the sheets, then store them in an airtight container in a cool, dry place for up to a month.

Shared at the table with…

189 ▸ SPRING

PART FOUR

SUMMER

Mozzarella with Tomatoes, Cucumbers, and Pesto

MAKES 12 APPETIZERS

This is an easy-to-prepare appetizer that looks fantastic and festive on a platter. And Rose Marie adds, "It's red, white, and green—the colors of the Italian flag!"
On the farm we make pesto using whatever green leaf we have in abundance, and have made this recipe using spinach, dandelion, arugula, and even nasturtium leaves. In this version we've used basil and parsley, but feel free to get creative.

>>>> *Shared at the table with...* <<<<

_____

_____

_____

_____

12 small mozzarella balls (bocconcini) or, if you can't find bocconcini, cut regular mozzarella into 1-inch cubes

1 tablespoon plus ½ cup Basil and Parsley Pesto (next page)

12 cherry tomatoes, halved

12 unpeeled cucumber slices, ¼ inch thick

12 small fresh basil leaves

12 small wooden skewers

Toss mozzarella in 1 tablespoon of pesto. Fill each skewer with one bocconcini, two tomato halves, one cucumber slice, and one basil leaf. Serve with the remaining ½ cup pesto on the side.

BASIL AND PARSLEY PESTO

MAKES 6 TO 8 SERVINGS

2 cups fresh basil leaves

½ cup fresh parsley

2 garlic cloves

2 tablespoons pine nuts

1 teaspoon kosher salt

½ cup extra-virgin olive oil

3 tablespoons butter, room temperature

½ cup grated Parmigiano cheese

3 tablespoons grated Pecorino Romano cheese

In a food processor, pulse basil, parsley, garlic, pine nuts, and salt until coarsely chopped. With the processor running, slowly pour the oil through the feed tube, stopping once or twice to scrape the sides down. Add the butter and pulse until well combined. Transfer to a bowl and stir in the Parmigiano and Pecorino. Transfer to refrigerator container, cover, and refrigerate.

To freeze, pour the pesto into ice cube trays and cover with plastic wrap. Once frozen solid (about 6 hours), you can remove cubes from the tray and store them in a freezer bag.

When we are harvesting our basil, we like to make multiple batches of this basic pesto and freeze it into cubes in an ice tray (you can also pour into small zipper-type bags and freeze flat). The pesto makes for a really quick dinner on those nights when work or farm chores have kept us from getting into the kitchen until late. Prepare your pasta and add the frozen pesto as soon as the pasta is drained. The pesto will melt and coat the pasta for an easy, quick, and delicious meal.

Goat Cheese–Filled Cherry Poppers

MAKES 24 POPPERS

These little poppers are packed full of both taste and texture, and you can vary the flavor by the type of pepper you use. In this recipe, we've used sweet cherry peppers, but feel free to experiment using different types of small peppers. Throw in a few habaneros if you like it hot. If you use different types of peppers, you can arrange them on your serving tray from mildest to wildest.

>>>——> *Shared at the* ←——<<<
table with…

_____

_____

_____

_____

¼ pound soft goat cheese

1 tablespoon finely chopped parsley

1 garlic clove, minced

½ teaspoon salt

¼ teaspoon white pepper

24 sweet cherry peppers, stem ends and any seeds removed

2 cups arugula

1 tablespoon olive oil

1½ teaspoons lemon juice

Salt and white pepper

In a small bowl mix together cheese, parsley, garlic, salt, and pepper.

Spoon cheese mixture into a resealable plastic bag and snip off a corner of the bag. Squeeze cheese filling into each pepper. Toss arugula with olive oil, lemon juice, and salt and pepper to taste. Arrange arugula on a serving platter and place filled peppers on top.

Fried Peppers with Balsamic Drizzle

**MAKES 8 SERVINGS AS AN APPETIZER
AND 4 SERVINGS AS A SIDE DISH**

1 pound mixed sweet mini peppers (using a variety of colored peppers will make this dish more festive)

¼ cup olive oil

2 garlic cloves, smashed

¼ cup fresh basil leaves, chopped

Salt and pepper

Beekman 1802 Whyte Drizzle (you can substitute white balsamic vinegar)

This colorful and delicious sweet pepper dish is not only a good appetizer; it also works well as a topping for bruschetta or as a side dish with grilled Italian sausages (see Fire-Pit Grilled Sausages and Potatoes, page 56).

Wash peppers and blot dry. Cut the peppers in half lengthwise and discard seeds and stems. In a large skillet, heat oil over low heat. Add the garlic and cook until a very pale golden color; be careful not to overcook or the garlic may become bitter. Add the peppers and basil, increase heat to medium, and cover the pan. Cook 5 minutes and stir. Add salt and pepper to taste and continue to cook uncovered for about 3 minutes or until done to your liking. Transfer to a serving plate and drizzle with the Whyte Drizzle. Serve at room temperature as part of an antipasto.

>>>>> *Shared at the table with…* <<<<<

_____

_____

_____

_____

Quick Pickled Vegetables

MAKES APPROXIMATELY 1 PINT

Doug and Garth are the proprietors of the famed American Hotel on Main Street. They were the very first people we met when we happened to travel through Sharon Springs and likely responsible for setting in motion the chain of events that would lead us to buy Beekman 1802 Farm and change our lives forever. We've spent many an evening eating and drinking at the hotel since. When we visit, the first treat that is placed on the table is a small bowl of pickled vegetables. The tart and sweet flavor wakes up the taste buds for everything to come.

Thanks for the inspiration, Doug and Garth. You will always have a seat at our table.

Shared at the table with...

_____

_____

_____

_____

_____

1 cup white wine vinegar

3 tablespoons sugar

1 tablespoon kosher salt

Additional spices (optional)

2 cups (about 1 pound) bite-sized vegetables (radishes, peppers, cauliflower, green tomatoes, or carrots)

Wash canning jars and lids or any other heatproof container that has an airtight lid, submerge containers in a saucepan of boiling water and boil for a couple of minutes to sterilize; drain.

In a small saucepan, bring 1 cup of water, the vinegar, sugar, and salt to a boil over high heat, stirring to dissolve the sugar.

If you are using spices, place them in the bottom of jars and fill the jar with vegetables. You can combine more than one vegetable in the same jar; just make sure the combined vegetables complement each other. Pour the hot brine over the vegetables to cover. Seal with the lid, turn upside down, and let cool to room temperature. Refrigerate.

The vegetables are ready to eat in a few hours. They'll keep up to 3 months in the refrigerator.

SOME VEGETABLE COMBOS
TO GET YOU STARTED

- Cauliflower, red pepper, and onion

- Cucumber, onion, zucchini, and garlic

- Asparagus and garlic scapes

- Carrots and radishes

Zucchini Blossoms with Savory Ricotta

MAKES 24 APPETIZERS

24 zucchini blossoms

2 cups ricotta

½ cup shredded mozzarella

¼ cup grated Pecorino Romano

1 tablespoon chopped fresh Italian parsley

Dash of nutmeg

Salt and pepper

1 cup all-purpose flour

1 tablespoon chopped fresh parsley

¼ teaspoon garlic powder

1 cup cold seltzer or club soda

Vegetable oil for frying

To prepare the blossoms, gently open each and remove the pistil. Gently wash the blossoms, if necessary, and drain well on paper towels. In a bowl, mix together the ricotta, mozzarella, Pecorino, parsley, nutmeg, and salt and pepper to taste. Fill each blossom with about 1 teaspoon of filling (depending on the size of the blossom). Gently close the blossom. Place the blossoms on a platter.

To prepare the batter, in a large bowl, mix together the flour, parsley, garlic powder, and salt and pepper to taste. Slowly add seltzer and mix until you have a smooth pancake-like batter; set aside.

In a large skillet, pour enough oil to come ⅛ inch up the side of the pan and heat over medium-high heat. When the oil is hot but not smoking, dip each blossom into the batter, allowing any excess to drip back into the bowl; gently place the blossom in the hot oil. Don't overcrowd the pan, which can lower the oil temperature and make the blossoms soggy. Cook until golden brown—1 to 2 minutes per side. When finished cooking, place blossoms on a paper towel–lined plate to drain, then sprinkle with salt. Serve warm.

Note: If you have any leftovers, you can store them in the refrigerator and heat them gently in a toaster oven.

Any gardener or farmer will tell you that there's always enough zucchini, so no need to worry about plucking a few of the blossoms. If you are harvesting from your own plants, pick the blossoms early in the morning to avoid the bees that enjoy nestling inside the flowers to get at the pollen. Squash grows from the female blossom, so if you are concerned about decreasing your squash yield, harvest only the male blossoms—the ones that contain the long pistil. Most farmers' markets and larger grocery stores carry zucchini blossoms when they're in season.

⟫⟫⟫ *Shared at the table with...* ⟪⟪⟪

_____

_____

_____

_____

Orange-Fennel Salad

MAKES 4 SERVINGS

Fresh fennel has a mild licorice taste, and when paired with citrus it makes this easy salad a perfect way to start any meal. The salad works especially well with grilled fish or chicken.

⟫⟫⟫ *Shared at the table with...* ⟪⟪⟪

1 large fennel bulb

½ small red onion, thinly sliced

2 large navel oranges

3 tablespoons extra-virgin olive oil

1 tablespoon lemon juice

Sea salt

Freshly cracked black pepper

Mint leaves (left whole) for garnish

Cut off and discard the fennel stalks and tough outer leaves from the bulb. Wash, dry, and thinly slice the fennel bulb. Chop the tender inner fronds. Place the fennel in a large serving bowl along with the onion.

Using a sharp knife, slice off both ends of each orange. Following the curve of the fruit, cut away the peel and white pith.

Working over a bowl to catch any juice, cut between the membranes to remove the segments from the oranges; these cut orange sections are called supremes. Add the orange supremes and juice to the bowl with the fennel. Squeeze the remaining orange pulp over the fennel to release any additional juices.

Add oil, lemon juice, and salt and pepper to taste. Toss gently to combine. Garnish with mint leaves.

KIP

THE FIRST TIME WE DROVE THROUGH THE MOHAWK VALLEY, we got lost. We drove by an old barn on the side of the road with acres of furniture, statuary, and old machinery weathering in the surrounding pasture. Inside, the barn was filled to the rafters with things. We were mesmerized and spent three hours walking about before getting back into our car to complete the trip to New York City.

After we moved to the farm, we often wondered about this place. The country roads are so twisting and turning and often so desolate that unless you've paid attention you might never find your way back to the same spot. It took us three years of living on the farm full time before fate took us down this road again.

Kip and his wife Judith are the owners of Wood Bull Antiques. They were both former students of the Rhode Island School of Design and are probably the most creative people we've ever met.

When we built the dining room table for the farmhouse, we needed 14 chairs to place around it. Kip climbed up to the top of the barn, walked across the beams as sure-footed as if he were on the ground, and in a matter of minutes sat 18 chairs on the ground for us to look it.

Those mismatched green chairs still play host to everyone who sits down to dinner with us at the farm (and you can even see them in some of the photos in this book), and you can find some of Kip's best vintage pieces in our own Mercantile in Sharon Springs.

Kip knows he's invited to our table at any time, but he also knows that we'd be just as happy sitting down at one of his.

Star Baby Soup

4 cups chicken broth

½ cup star pastina

1 tablespoon grated Parmigiano cheese

4 ice cubes (optional)

In a medium saucepan, bring broth to a simmer over medium heat. Add pastina and cook 4 to 6 minutes or until tender. Add cheese and stir. Ladle soup into soup bowls. If desired, serve with an ice cube in each bowl to quickly cool the soup.

In Italy, pastina (tiny star-shaped pasta) is the first solid food fed to babies. It's still comfort food for Rose Marie's daughters; they now make it themselves when they're not feeling well. This soup right off the stove is too hot for a small child; just add ice cubes to cool it quickly. The kids will love watching the ice cubes melt away. This is a quick and easy soup to make whenever you need a little TLC and there's no one else around to give it to you. Love yourself!

Shared at the table with…

Christian's Lentil Soup

MAKES 6 TO 8 CUPS

We found photographer Christian Watson, who shot the stunning photos for this book, on Instagram. He shoots only in natural light—a departure from the way most cookbooks are shot—and, at the age of 23, had never photographed a cookbook before. Just like our small community supported us as we grew, Beekman 1802 pays it forward by identifying artisans and challenging them to apply their talents in ways they may have never thought. It was no time at all after we first met to discuss this project that Christian became a "neighbor." He came up with the title of his first book of photography, Every Small Town Smells Like Hickory, while sitting on a park bench on his first night in Sharon Springs.

Christian loves camping and being alone in the wilderness, and he fell in love with this soup. We hope that it will always bring him comfort and warmth no matter where his life and travels take him.

Shared at the table with…

2 tablespoons olive oil

2 slices pancetta or smoked ham, diced (optional)

1 small onion, chopped

2 cloves garlic, chopped

1 stalk celery with leaves, chopped

1 carrot, diced

1 pound lentils, rinsed and drained

4 plum tomatoes, diced

2 bay leaves

2 bouillon cubes: chicken, beef, or vegetable

Salt and pepper

In a large pot, heat oil over medium heat. Add pancetta, onion, garlic, celery, and carrot and cook, stirring occasionally until onion is golden—about 5 minutes. Add lentils, tomatoes, bay leaves, bouillon, 8 cups of water, and salt and pepper to taste; bring to a boil. Reduce to a simmer, cover, and cook until the lentils are tender and the soup is thick—45 minutes. Add more water to thin the soup, if you want, and adjust salt and pepper if necessary. Remove the bay leaves.

If you want to make this dish with pasta, cook and drain a pound of *ditalini*, small shells, or your favorite short pasta until it's al dente; drain and mix with lentils.

Note: You can replace the water and bouillon cubes with 8 cups of chicken stock.

Breakfast of Champions Pizza Dough

MAKES 2 PORTIONS OF DOUGH, 1 POUND EACH

Brent loves pizza for breakfast—hot or cold. One morning he woke up around 5 A.M., and posted on Facebook, "Those sad mornings when you know there's no pizza to eat." He went upstairs to take a shower and get ready for the day. Thirty minutes later he came back downstairs and on the kitchen table was a pizza. Rose Marie had snuck in and put it there!

Rose Marie always has frozen pizza dough on hand. When she makes pizza dough, she makes a double batch, using one and freezing the other. This recipe makes enough dough for 2 pizzas, each using a 14-inch round pizza pan. This dough is also perfect for the Tomato Pie on page 212.

>>>> *Shared at the* <<<<
table with…

2 cups warm water	2 tablespoons olive oil
2½ teaspoons active dry yeast	5½ cups unbleached all-purpose flour
½ teaspoon sugar	1½ teaspoons salt

Combine water, yeast, sugar, and oil in a measuring cup with a pouring spout. Let stand 5 minutes or until foamy.

Place 5 cups of the flour in the bowl of a food processor. Add the salt and pulse to mix. With the machine running, pour yeast mixture through feed tube and pulse to combine. When thoroughly mixed, add the remaining ½ cup of flour and pulse until the dough comes together and forms a ball. Remove the dough and place in a large oiled bowl. Cover with plastic wrap and let rise in a warm, draft-free spot until double in size—about 1½ hours. Placing the covered bowl in the oven with only the light on will speed up the rising process. Divide dough into two balls.

If you choose to freeze the dough, place it in a resealable plastic freezer bag. Use a straw to draw all the air from the bag to prevent freezer burn. When you are ready to use this dough later, defrost it overnight in the refrigerator. Let the dough come to room temperature before using.

Raw Tomato Sauce

MAKES ABOUT 2 CUPS OF SAUCE

2 pounds ripe plum tomatoes, cored, halved, and seeded

2 garlic cloves, finely minced

12 large basil leaves

¼ cup fresh parsley

½ cup extra-virgin olive oil

Salt and pepper

In a food processor, pulse the tomatoes, garlic, basil, and parsley until the tomatoes are coarsely chopped. Transfer to a bowl, add the oil, and season with salt and pepper to taste. Cover with plastic wrap and set aside.

The sauce may be left out for several hours. It keeps in the refrigerator up to 3 days. Return to room temperature before using.

In peak summer, the tomatoes are bountiful and no one wants to spend a day at a hot stove cooking sauce. This sauce captures the best essence of the tomato—and you make it all in your blender or food processor! Toss this sauce with a pound of your favorite pasta and sprinkle with Pecorino Romano, or use it on grilled Italian bread or bruschetta.

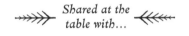

Shared at the table with…

Tomato Pie

2 tablespoons olive oil

1 pound Breakfast of Champions Pizza Dough (page 208) or store-bought pizza dough

½ cup shredded mozzarella

½ cup tomato sauce or pizza sauce

2 to 4 heirloom tomatoes, cored and sliced (it's nice to vary the color and size)

1 tablespoon grated Parmigiano cheese

1 teaspoon dried oregano

Black pepper

Move a rack to the middle position in the oven and preheat the oven to 450°F.

Rub a 12-inch springform pan with 1 tablespoon of oil. Place the dough in the pan and press it in the bottom and up the sides of the pan to just beneath the rim. Push your fingertips into the dough to make indentations. Sprinkle half the mozzarella over the dough, then the sauce, and then the remaining mozzarella.

Arrange the sliced tomatoes on top of the mozzarella and sprinkle with Parmigiano and oregano, then drizzle with the remaining tablespoon of oil and sprinkle with pepper to taste.

Cover and let rise for 30 minutes.

Bake 25 to 30 minutes.

Maria was the very first employee we hired. In those first years of Beekman 1802 Mercantile, we would work 18-hour days. She became a friend, a confidante, and a person who could easily throw a wrench into the rumor mill that is so much a part of small-town life. As the business grew, she brought in her husband, Pete, a retired dairy farmer, and he now is a critical component of our shipping operations. Without the two of them, there would be no Beekman 1802. They will always have a seat at the table.

Maria and Pete are notoriously picky eaters, but even they love this recipe. It's pure comfort food—Italian style.

$\ggg$ *Shared at the table with…* $\lll$

Grilled Summer Vegetables

MAKES 6 TO 8 SERVINGS

There's a small church just down the road from Beekman Farm, and it is the same church that William Beekman attended in the early 1800s. He even paid for the bell that rang out through the valley every Sunday. During the summer, the current members of that church bring anything they have in excess from their gardens and put it in a makeshift wooden stand by the side of the road. Everything on the stand is free for anyone in need of something fresh and nutritious.

It's always been true that farming communities share the bounty. One of the ways we like to cook up our good fortune is by throwing everything into a pouch of tin foil and tossing it on the grill.

This method is so versatile; you may use any combination of vegetables that are in season. Remember to use vegetables that have about the same cooking time. If you've got sprigs of rosemary, thyme, or sage leaves, toss them into the mixture, too.

>>> *Shared at the* <<<
table with...

_____

_____

_____

_____

2 medium zucchini, cut into 2-inch spears

1 medium eggplant, cut into pieces about 1 inch thick by 3 inches long

1 small red onion, cut into ¼-inch slices

1 green bell pepper, cut into ¾-inch strips

1 red bell pepper, cut into ¾-inch strips

2 large tomatoes, cut into 1-inch-wide wedges

2 cloves garlic, minced

2 tablespoons olive oil

¼ teaspoon kosher salt

Black pepper

Cooking spray

¼ cup grated Pecorino Romano cheese

In a large bowl, toss together zucchini, eggplant, onion, bell peppers, tomatoes, and garlic. Add the oil, salt, and pepper to taste and toss until everything is well coated.

Lay two large sheets of heavy-duty foil on top of each other to make a double layer of foil. Spray the top foil sheet with cooking spray. Place vegetables on one half of the foil. Sprinkle cheese over the vegetables. Fold the foil in half and fold up the sides of the foil to seal.

Heat a grill to high heat. Grill vegetables for about 10 minutes on each side or until tender. To serve, carefully cut a slit in the foil to release steam, and serve directly from the foil pack, or move to a serving dish.

Pasta Substitutes

EACH MAKES 4 SERVINGS

We have friends who are pasta lovers but either are gluten intolerant or vegans. Of course you can buy gluten-free pasta at the supermarket, but you can also make a vegetable version yourself that's healthy, satisfies a craving, and does just as well supporting whatever sauce you make.

>>>>> *Shared at the table with...* <<<<<

BAKED SPAGHETTI SQUASH "NOODLES"

1 (2- to 3-pound) spaghetti squash

Preheat the oven to 400°F. Place the squash in a baking dish and use a paring knife to pierce it in several places. Pour ½ cup water into the pan.

Cover with foil and bake 1 hour or until a fork can easily pierce the squash. Uncover and let it cool. Cut the squash in half horizontally and discard the seeds and stringy flesh. Scrape the squash into "noodles" by pulling a fork down the length of the inside of the squash.

If you want the "noodles" a bit more dressed, toss them with 1 tablespoon olive oil and flavor with salt and pepper to taste.

Top the prepared noodles with your favorite sauce.

ZUCCHINI "NOODLES"

4 small zucchini

Wash, trim, and halve zucchini lengthwise. Cut each half into thin strips the length of the zucchini. Alternatively, use a vegetable peeler to make ribbons of zucchini or use a mandolin to create fettuccine, spaghetti, or pappardelle shaped "noodles." To make more noodle-like noodles, process the zucchini in a vegetable spiral slicer.

To sauté the "noodles," in a medium-size pan over medium heat, heat 2 tablespoons olive oil. Add the zucchini "noodles" and sauté for about 3 minutes. Season with salt and pepper to taste.

To boil the "noodles," drop them into salted boiling water for 1 minute, drain.

Top the prepared noodles with your favorite sauce.

A SUMMER GARDEN PARTY

WE LIVE OUR LIFE ON THE FARM by the season and try as much as possible to celebrate what every season brings us.

The goats are bred during the late fall and start kidding (having their babies) around March. The first flush of milk means that we start production of cheese for the year and serves as a signal to us that it's time for the farm—and all of its inhabitants—to wake up from the long winter hibernation.

We start our seeds in the cellar and plant them outdoors after the last frost; by the time the first wheels of cheese are ready to come out of the aging cave in July, the vegetable garden is usually just starting to reveal its bounty.

We built a harvesting table that sits in the very center of the vegetable garden. It was initially meant for us to lay our tools and our vegetables on so that they could be easily cleaned using the watering hose, but just as often now this humble workhorse serves as the hub for many a summer gathering of neighbors.

On this particular evening three people who had never been to the farm happened to stop by. Although they live in New York City and Connecticut, they're still neighbors to us.

It turns out that one of them happens to work for chef Anthony Bourdain, which proves that you just never know who you are going to meet when you invite someone to gather 'round your table.

Garden Party Menu

A wheel of Beekman 1802 Blaak goat cheese

A button of Beekman 1802 Fresh Chèvre

Soppressata

Olive Salad
(PAGE 89)

Goat Cheese–Filled Cherry Poppers
(PAGE 194)

Mozzarella with Tomatoes, Cucumbers, and Pesto
(PAGE 192)

Bacon-Wrapped Stuffed Dates
(PAGE 85)

Grilled Pizza
(BREAKFAST OF CHAMPIONS PIZZA DOUGH, PAGE 208)

Field Greens, Fig, and Brie Salad
(PAGE 141)

Potato Frittata

MAKES 6 SERVINGS

1 pound potatoes, peeled and sliced ¼ inch thick

¼ cup olive oil

1 large onion, halved and thinly sliced

6 large eggs

½ cup grated Pecorino Romano cheese

1 tablespoon chopped fresh parsley

⅛ teaspoon grated nutmeg

½ teaspoon salt

⅛ teaspoon black pepper

In a large pot of salted boiling water, cook the potatoes until tender—8 minutes. Drain and set aside to cool.

In a 10-inch nonstick skillet, heat oil over medium heat and cook the onion until translucent—7 minutes.

In a large bowl, mix together the eggs, cheese, parsley, nutmeg, salt, and pepper. Add the potatoes and gently mix. Pour mixture into the skillet. Shake the pan to distribute the eggs evenly. Cover and cook 10 minutes on medium heat. Shake pan from time to time to prevent sticking.

Place a heatproof plate over the skillet and flip the frittata over onto the plate. Slide the frittata back into the pan and continue to cook uncovered until it's set and golden on the bottom—10 minutes. Slide the frittata onto a serving plate. (We do this step over the sink or a clean cutting board—just in case!) Cut into wedges and serve.

The farm chores are endless during harvest season, and this frittata is a perfect meal during that busy time. The frittata is easy to prepare and provides many hours of sustenance. Maybe even until the cows come home.

>>>>> *Shared at the table with…* <<<<<

_____

_____

_____

_____

Linguine with Lemon Sauce

MAKES 6 SERVINGS

Lemons are abundant in Sicily, and like any bumper crop, when you have a lot of something, you find creative uses for it. Sicilians use lemons to do everything from cleaning their flatware and cleansing their skin to creating or enhancing delicious meals by adding the zest and juice. Here lemons are used to make a bright sauce for this irresistible pasta dish.

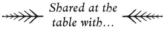

Shared at the table with...

1 pound linguine

8 tablespoons unsalted butter

Zest and juice from 1 large lemon

½ teaspoon salt

¼ teaspoon white pepper

⅓ cup fresh basil leaves, julienned

½ cup heavy cream

¾ cup freshly grated Parmigiano cheese, plus more for serving

½ cup toasted pine nuts (you can substitute chopped toasted pistachios)

Fresh basil for garnish

In a large pot of boiling salted water, cook the linguine until al dente and drain, reserving ½ cup of the pasta water.

Meanwhile, in a large skillet, melt the butter over medium-low heat. Add the zest, juice, salt, pepper, ⅓ cup basil, and the cream. Stir and heat gently 1 minute to blend the flavors. Add the cooked linguine and the grated cheese to the pan, and toss until the linguine is evenly coated. If the linguine is too dry for your taste, add a little of the pasta water. Serve in warm pasta bowls and garnish with toasted pine nuts and additional basil. Sprinkle more grated cheese at the table.

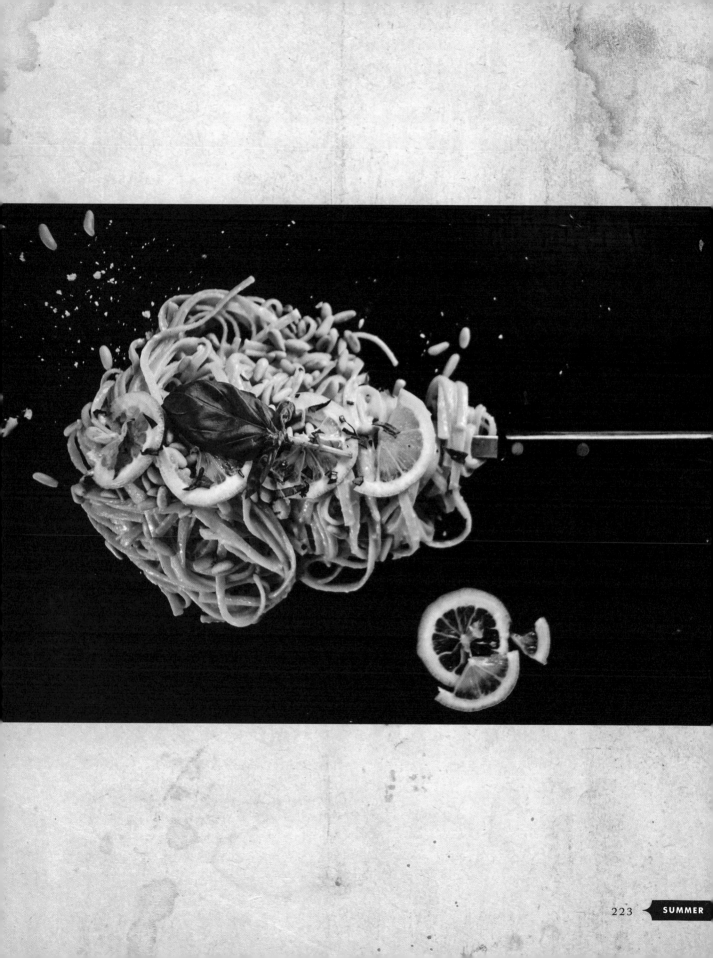

Perciatelli (Hollow) Pasta with Fennel and Sardines

MAKES 4 SERVINGS

If you look at the record books from Ellis Island, many immigrants came with seeds in their pockets. Rose Marie brought back wild fennel seeds from Sicily and planted them in her garden in Sharon Springs so that she could make this family heirloom recipe EXACTLY the way her grandmother did.

This pasta sauce is traditionally served over long thick, hollow pasta strands known as perciatelli *or* bucatini*. If you can't find either, you can substitute spaghetti. The dish traditionally includes fried sardines, but you can leave them out if they're not to your taste. Regardless of whether you use sardines, the toasted breadcrumbs provide added texture to the dish.*

>>>> *Shared at the table with...* <<<<

_____

_____

_____

_____

1 fennel bulb, stalks discarded, fronds finely chopped (about 2 cups once all sliced and chopped)

8 ounces perciatelli pasta (also known as bucatini)

½ cup olive oil

1 clove garlic, finely chopped

½ small red onion, thinly sliced

2 anchovy fillets, finely chopped

2 tablespoons chopped fresh parsley

¼ teaspoon red pepper flakes

¾ teaspoon salt

2 cups plain breadcrumbs

2 bay leaves

8 turns of black pepper mill

¼ cup sugar

Hard grating cheese (such as ricotta salata or Pecorino Romano), for garnish

Fried Sardines (optional, recipe on next page)

Cut the fennel bulb in half lengthwise, discard the tough outer layer and thinly slice bulb.

In a large pot of boiling salted water, cook the sliced fennel and pasta until the pasta is al dente. Drain, reserving 1 cup of the pasta cooking water. Transfer to a large bowl and cover to keep warm.

In a small saucepan, heat ¼ cup of the oil over medium-low heat. Add the garlic, onion, anchovies, parsley, pepper flakes, and ½ teaspoon salt. Cook, stirring occasionally, until the onion is tender. Set aside.

In a large skillet, heat the remaining ¼ cup oil over medium heat. Add the breadcrumbs, bay leaves, remaining ¼ teaspoon salt, and the pepper. Cook, stirring occasionally, until the breadcrumbs are golden brown. Don't leave

the pan unattended because the breadcrumbs can burn very quickly. Remove from the heat, add the sugar, and mix. Remove the bay leaves and discard.

Add the chopped fennel fronds and the oil and onion mixture to the bowl with the pasta, toss well, and serve with toasted breadcrumbs, grated hard cheese, and if using, fried sardines.

FRIED SARDINES

½ cup all-purpose flour

¼ teaspoon salt

⅛ teaspoon black pepper

8 fresh sardines, cleaned (heads and bones removed), butterflied and dry

Olive oil, for frying

On a large plate, season flour with salt and pepper. Coat sardines in flour mixture and shake off excess. In a large skillet, pour oil to ⅛ inch depth and heat over medium-high heat. Fry the sardines until golden brown—about 2 minutes on each side; drain on paper towels.

Brown-Sugared Pork Ribs
with Bourbon BBQ Sauce

MAKES 4 SERVINGS

The very first meal we ever cooked for our neighbors in Sharon Springs was a summer barbecue, and that's where the recipe for our famous Mortgage Lifter Bourbon barbecue first started taking shape. You can make this recipe using our Mortgage Lifter sauce, your own favorite barbecue sauce, or even without sauce—using only the eye-opening, mouth-watering rub. Your choice.

>>>>> *Shared at the table with...* <<<<<

_____

_____

_____

_____

BROWN SUGAR RUB

1 cup packed brown sugar

1 tablespoon kosher salt

1½ tablespoons sweet paprika

1 tablespoon black pepper

1 tablespoon garlic powder

1 tablespoon onion powder

1 tablespoon instant espresso powder

½ tablespoon chili powder

1 teaspoon oregano

½ teaspoon red pepper flakes

1 large (4-pound) rack of pork ribs

1 cup Beekman 1802 Mortgage Lifter Bourbon barbecue sauce or your favorite barbecue sauce (optional)

First, make the brown sugar rub. This recipe makes about 1½ cups of rub, and you only use ¼ cup for this recipe, so you'll have plenty to store and use for future barbecues. To make the rub, in a medium bowl, stir together all of the rub ingredients. Scoop out ¼ cup of rub to use for the ribs; store the rest in a lidded jar.

Now rinse the ribs with cold water and pat dry with paper towels. Cut the membrane from the underside of the ribs and pull it off. This step is optional, but because the membrane is chewy and doesn't cook as the meat does, removing it makes the ribs easy to eat.

Season the ribs with the reserved ¼ cup of rub, rubbing it into both sides of the rack. Place the ribs on a heavy duty foil–lined large rimmed baking sheet. Let the ribs sit at room temperature for at least 30 minutes so that the rub penetrates the meat. You may also let the ribs, covered in rub, marinate overnight in the refrigerator.

Preheat the oven to 300°F. Heat a grill to high. When the grill has reached temperature, grill the rack for 15 minutes per side. (Alternatively, you can broil the rack in the oven for 15 minutes per side on the same baking sheet you'll use for the baking.) Return the ribs to the baking sheet, cover tightly with foil, and bake for 2 hours. Uncover the ribs and baste with barbecue sauce, if you're using it. Now set the oven to broil, and cook the ribs 6 inches from heat until the sauce caramelizes—3 minutes. Be careful not to burn the ribs.

Remove the ribs from the oven, and cut them between bones. Serve with additional sauce.

Spiced Pork Tenderloin with Warm Orzo Salad

MAKES 8 SERVINGS

Brent loves leftovers (and Rose Marie loves to feed them to him). This pork is delicious served with a warm orzo salad, but it's equally delicious the next day served as a sandwich with the meat dripping from a Chinese-style steamed rice bun or a soft roll. The orzo salad is also great served as a cold salad.

>>>>>> *Shared at the table with...* <<<<<<

_____

_____

_____

_____

Two 1-pound pork tenderloins

¼ cup sweet bean paste

3 tablespoons hoisin sauce

1 tablespoon ketchup

½ teaspoon garlic powder

¼ teaspoon five-spice powder

3 tablespoons dark soy sauce

1 tablespoon white wine

1 whole star anise

¼ cup rock sugar (you may substitute light brown sugar)

Orzo Salad (next page)

Wash pork; dry with paper towels. In a small bowl, mix together the bean paste, hoisin, ketchup, garlic powder, and five-spice powder. Rub the pork all over with the bean paste mixture, cover and marinate for at least 2 hours in the refrigerator.

In a pot large enough to hold the pork, bring 1 cup of water and the soy sauce, wine, and star anise to a boil. Add the pork, reduce to a gentle simmer, cover, and cook 30 minutes.

Add the sugar, cover, and simmer 1 more hour, turning frequently.

When the sauce is reduced to ½ cup and is rather thick like syrup, remove the pan from the heat and let the pork cool in the pot for 10 minutes. Slice the pork, arrange attractively on a platter, and pour the sauce over. Serve with Orzo Salad.

ORZO SALAD

MAKES 8 SERVINGS

1 pound orzo pasta

1 red bell pepper, cut into small dice

6 scallions, thinly sliced

2 garlic cloves, minced

½ cup chopped fresh Italian parsley

½ cup chopped cilantro

1 cup Thai-style sweet chile sauce

Juice of 2 limes

3 tablespoons mirin (sweetened rice wine)

1 tablespoon white wine

1 stalk lemongrass, minced

1 teaspoon freshly grated ginger

1 cup roasted cashews

1 tablespoon black sesame seeds

Cook orzo according to package directions; drain well and transfer to a large glass serving bowl. Add the remaining ingredients and toss to combine. Serve warm or at room temperature.

Chicken Cacciatore alla Fortunata

MAKES 6 TO 8 SERVINGS

Fortunata (which means "fortunate") is the maiden name of Rose Marie's mother-in-law. When she made this dish, one of her signatures, she would reserve some of the sauce and serve it over linguini as a first course.

>>>>> *Shared at the table with...* <<<<<

4 tablespoons olive oil

1 large onion, halved and thinly sliced

⅓ cup finely diced carrots

½ cup finely diced celery

¼ teaspoon red pepper flakes

2 garlic cloves, minced

2 sprigs fresh rosemary

¼ cup chopped fresh parsley

One 14.5-ounce can of diced tomatoes

One 4- to 5-pound chicken, carved into 12 pieces (2 legs, 2 thighs, 2 wings, 2 breasts, 4 back pieces), or alternatively use 6 chicken breasts

Salt and pepper

½ cup Marsala wine

1 green bell pepper, cut into ¾-inch-wide strips

½ large red bell pepper, cut into ¾-inch-wide strips

In a large Dutch oven, heat 3 tablespoons of the oil over medium heat. Add the onion, carrots, celery, red pepper flakes, and garlic. Cook, stirring occasionally, until the vegetables are a light golden color—5 minutes. Add the rosemary and parsley and cook for 2 minutes. Lower the heat to very low; add the tomatoes and ½ cup water and cook for 10 more minutes.

Meanwhile, in a large skillet, heat the remaining 1 table-spoon oil over medium heat and cook the chicken pieces until golden brown—about 5 minutes per side. To get a gorgeous brown color, do not move the chicken around as it cooks; let it brown, and then turn it over and brown the other side. Season with salt and pepper to taste. Pour the Marsala over the chicken and cook until the wine is reduced by half.

Place the chicken and Marsala on top of the onion-carrot-celery mixture in the Dutch oven.

Add the bell peppers to the pan the chicken cooked in and stir-fry for 3 to 4 minutes. Then add the peppers to the Dutch oven; cover and simmer over low heat until the chicken is tender—about 45 minutes. Remove the chicken to a serving platter and cover with foil to keep warm. Increase the heat to medium-high and reduce the sauce for about 5 minutes. Spoon some sauce over the chicken and serve the rest of the sauce on the side.

Chicken Breasts with Roasted Red Pepper, Gremolata, and Prosciutto

MAKES 4 SERVINGS

The parsley-arugula mixture known as gremolata is a great all-purpose condiment. Here we use it almost as a relish. It can be used as a dipping sauce by adding more olive oil and lemon juice. You can also use it on grilled meat and fish, toss it into vegetables, or use it as a spread for sandwiches.

Two 6- to 8-ounce boneless, skinless chicken breast halves

2 cups fresh Italian parsley

2 cups arugula

3 cloves garlic

Zest and juice of 1 lemon

½ cup extra-virgin olive oil

One 12-ounce jar roasted red peppers, drained and dried

6 thin slices provolone cheese

6 thin slices prosciutto

Salt and pepper

Preheat the oven to 375°F. Lightly grease a baking dish.

Place the chicken on a cutting board lined with paper towels. With your hand flat on top of one of the breasts and using a sharp knife, cut a lengthwise slit into the thickest side of the chicken breast to within ½ inch of the opposite side. Open the chicken like a book, so that it lies flat; cover with plastic wrap. Use the flat side of a meat mallet to flatten the chicken breast to ¼-inch thickness. Repeat with the second chicken breast.

To make the gremolata, in a food processor, pulse the parsley, arugula, and garlic until roughly chopped. Add the zest, juice, and oil and pulse to combine.

Spread gremolata on each butterflied chicken breast to within 1 inch of the long side of the chicken. Layer each piece with a single layer each of roasted peppers and provolone so that they are more or less the size of the prior layer. Roll up the long edge towards opposite side to enclose filling.

Place a large sheet of plastic wrap on a clean surface and slightly overlap slices of prosciutto so they're as wide as one rolled chicken breast. Set a rolled breast at one end of the prosciutto. Roll prosciutto tightly around the breast. Repeat with the second chicken breast. The prosciutto should completely cover the meat. You may need additional prosciutto depending on the size of the chicken rolls.

Place the chicken seam side down in the baking dish and bake 25 to 30 minutes. Remove the baking dish from the oven and let the chicken rest a few minutes before slicing. Serve with extra gremolata and salt and pepper to taste.

Baked Salmon with Tomato and Green Peppercorn Butter

MAKES 8 SERVINGS

Serve this with a side of Cucumber-Dill Salad (recipe on next page). If you like, make an extra batch of tomato and green peppercorn butter, shape it into a log, wrap it in plastic wrap, and store it in the freezer. You can serve this butter on grilled steak.

⇶⇶⇶ *Shared at the table with...* ⇷⇷⇷

Cooking spray

1 garlic clove, chopped

1 teaspoon fresh rosemary leaves

2 tablespoons green peppercorns in vinegar, drained and rinsed

2 sun-dried tomatoes in oil, drained

¼ teaspoon salt

Zest and juice of 1 lemon

8 tablespoons unsalted butter, room temperature

1 tablespoon olive oil

1 whole side (3 pounds) skin-on salmon fillet, scaled, rinsed, and pin bones removed

½ cup panko bread crumbs

Preheat the oven to 425°F. Line a rimmed baking sheet with heavy-duty foil and spray with cooking spray.

In a food processor, pulse the garlic, rosemary, peppercorns, tomatoes, salt, zest, and juice until finely chopped. Add the butter and oil and pulse until well blended. Use a spatula to transfer the butter to a bowl.

Wash the salmon under cold water and dry with paper towels. Place salmon skin-side down on the prepared baking sheet. Generously cover the salmon with the butter mixture and sprinkle evenly with breadcrumbs, pressing to adhere. Bake 15 minutes.

You may serve with skin side down on the plate or, using a spatula, gently lift the meat of the fish away from the skin before serving.

CUCUMBER-DILL SALAD

MAKES 8 SERVINGS

3 large cucumbers, thinly sliced

1 tablespoon kosher salt

1 cup sugar

½ cup distilled white vinegar

3 tablespoons fresh lemon juice

½ cup thinly sliced red onion

3 tablespoons chopped fresh dill or 1 tablespoon dried dill weed

In a large bowl, sprinkle the cucumbers with salt and toss to coat. Cover with a weighted plate and let sit for 1 hour. Transfer to a colander; rinse well, drain, and pat dry. In a large serving bowl, whisk together the sugar, vinegar, ½ cup water, and the lemon juice until the sugar has dissolved. Add the cucumbers, onion, and dill. Refrigerate at least 3 hours to allow the flavors to blend.

Scallops Caprese

MAKES 6 SERVINGS

Josh loves scallops because they look like little packages on the plate, and they are one of the easiest types of seafood to prepare.

→→→ *Shared at the table with...* ←←←

_____

_____

_____

_____

2 pounds heirloom tomatoes

24 fresh basil leaves

3 medium red onions, sliced 1 inch thick

Kosher salt and pepper

6 tablespoons extra-virgin olive oil, plus extra for the pan

12 large dry diver scallops

Sea salt

1 lemon, halved

Slice the tomatoes creatively—some small ones whole, some in wedges. Arrange them on a platter. Tear basil over the tomatoes. Set aside.

Season onion with kosher salt and pepper to taste.

Heat an oiled cast-iron grill pan over high heat and cook the onions for 7 minutes. Do not move them; you want them to char evenly. Flip them and cook until they're charred and softened—another 7 to 10 minutes. Transfer to a plate to cool. Separate into rings and scatter them over the tomatoes.

Drizzle 4 tablespoons of oil over the tomatoes and onions.

Make sure that the scallops are dry. Cut a ¼-inch checkerboard pattern into one side of each scallop. Heat an oiled cast-iron skillet over medium-high heat and sear the scallops, design-side down, without moving the scallops, until almost cooked—5 to 7 minutes. Flip them and sear 30 seconds; overcooking will make the scallops tough and chewy. Arrange them on the salad. Season with the remaining 2 tablespoons of oil and sea salt to taste and squeeze lemon juice over the salad.

Peaches and Wine

6 SERVINGS

Life is short, so why not start with dessert first? This is an excellent cocktail-cum-dessert *recipe for those luxuriously long summer nights. When your guests arrive, fill their glasses with cut peaches and red wine. Throughout the evening and the course of dinner, continue to pour the wine over the peaches. The peaches in each cup will absorb the red wine throughout the meal. When the meal is over and it's time for dessert (or when the red wine runs out), pass around a bowl of whipped cream, mascarpone, or vanilla ice cream. A dollop to each glass and a spoon and you have a truly happy ending.*

6 peaches	1 bottle red wine
2 cloves	Peel from 1 lemon
2 tablespoons sugar	Mint sprigs for garnish

Wash and dry peaches. Slice them and place in a glass bowl with cloves, sugar, wine, and lemon peel. Refrigerate for 2 hours. Remove cloves and lemon peel and discard.

Divide peaches between six wine glasses and fill the glasses with the steeped wine. Garnish with mint.

When peaches aren't in season, you can substitute peeled oranges.

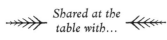

Shared at the table with…

_____

_____

_____

_____

Little Bits of Honey (*Struffoli*)

MAKES ABOUT 4 DOZEN

We've been keeping bees on the farm for more than 9 years—over 30 hives now—and during the late spring and summer, the world beyond our back porch has a palpable vibration from their constant work. Like so many things in life, it's hard to appreciate how much work goes into creating something truly special, but the bees are a constant reminder that nothing good comes easy.

These sweet bites make you aware of every drop of nectar and effort that goes into their making.

>>>>> *Shared at the table with…* <<<<<

_____

_____

_____

_____

_____

STRUFFOLI

4 large eggs

2 egg yolks

½ cup vegetable oil

½ cup sugar

2 tablespoons vanilla extract

4 cups all-purpose flour

½ teaspoon baking powder

Finely grated zest of 1 orange

4 cups vegetable oil

COATING

2 cups honey

½ cup sugar, plus more for sprinkling

Zest of 1 orange, cut into thin strips

Start by making the struffoli. In a large bowl, whisk together the eggs, egg yolks, oil, sugar, and vanilla. In a small bowl, stir together the flour, baking powder, and orange zest; add the egg mixture to the dry ingredients and knead with your hands to form a smooth dough. Transfer to a lightly floured wooden board, divide the dough into 16 equal pieces, and roll each piece into a pencil-thin rope. Cut each rope into ½-inch pieces and roll the pieces into small balls.

Pour the 4 cups of oil into a deep pot or fryer and heat to 375°F on a deep-fry thermometer. Working in batches, carefully drop a few struffoli into the oil and cook until golden brown—about 3 minutes. Drain on a paper towel–lined plate and allow to cool to room temperature.

Now make the coating for the struffoli. In a large skillet, heat 1 cup of the honey, ¼ cup of the sugar, and half the orange strips over medium heat until the sugar has dissolved and the mixture is bubbly. Add half of the room-temperature struffoli and gently stir to coat. With a slotted spoon, lift the struffoli out of the honey mixture

and transfer to a serving plate, mounding them on top of each other. Sprinkle with sugar. Repeat with the remaining struffoli, coating with the remaining honey, sugar, and orange zest, and sprinkling with more sugar.

Serve using forks or toothpicks or skip the formalities and just let people get their sticky little fingers on them.

In-a-Minute Icebox Lemon Semifreddo

MAKES 12 SERVINGS

24 Nilla Wafers cookies

One 14-ounce can sweetened condensed milk

3 large fresh eggs, separated

½ cup lemon juice

¼ teaspoon lemon extract

4 teaspoons sugar

1 cup heavy cream

Fresh berries, for serving

In a food processor, pulse the cookies to fine crumbs. Reserve 1 tablespoon for sprinkling on top. Coat the bottom of a 9-inch round metal cake pan with remaining cookie crumbs.

In a large bowl, whisk together the condensed milk, egg yolks, lemon juice, and lemon extract. In another bowl, beat the egg whites until soft peaks form. Add 3 teaspoons of the sugar and beat until stiff. Fold egg whites into condensed milk mixture. In a separate bowl, whip the heavy cream with the remaining teaspoon of sugar until soft peaks form; fold into the condensed milk mixture. Pour the mixture over the crumbs in the cake pan. Sprinkle with the reserved cookie crumbs. Cover with aluminum foil and freeze. Serve with fresh berries.

If you ever happen to find yourself at Rose Marie's house, you'll also find that within a minute she has something delicious sitting in front of you. One summer afternoon we stopped by her house to return some of her dishes, and before we could even say "thank you" we found ourselves sitting on her porch eating this refreshing dessert. It can be made ahead of time and kept in the freezer for weeks. It's very easy to slice off individual portions whenever company drops by. Warning: Once the word gets out, expect a lot of company.

→→→→ *Shared at the table with...* ←←←←

_____

_____

_____

_____

243 ◄ SUMMER

Plum and Peach Crostata

MAKES 8 SERVINGS

We were photographing this cookbook mid-summer. On a day that had been set aside to prepare the heavy meat dishes, we all found ourselves craving something sweet (of course!). The tree right outside the kitchen window was dripping with ripe plums. We pulled out a ball of dough we had been keeping in the freezer and within half an hour had satisfied everyone's sweet tooth.

→→→ *Shared at the table with...* ←←←

PASTRY CRUST

1½ cups all-purpose flour

2 tablespoons sugar

½ teaspoon salt

6 tablespoons cold butter, cut up

¼ cup ice water

FILLING

6 ripe Italian (prune) plums

4 large ripe peaches

¼ cup plus 2 tablespoons packed dark brown sugar

½ teaspoon vanilla extract

¼ teaspoon ground cinnamon

2 tablespoons all-purpose flour, plus more for the board

2 tablespoons heavy cream

2 tablespoons coarse sugar

Start by making the pastry crust. In a food processor, pulse the flour, sugar, and salt to combine. Add the butter and pulse until the butter is in pea-size pieces. Add the water and pulse just until the dough comes together. Place dough on a floured board and shape into a flat disk. Wrap in plastic wrap and refrigerate for 30 minutes.

Move an oven rack to the center position and preheat the oven to 425°F. Line a baking sheet with parchment paper.

Now make the filling. Cut plums and peaches into ½-inch slices, remove the pits, and place in a bowl. Add brown sugar, vanilla, cinnamon, and flour and toss to coat. Set aside. On a lightly floured board, roll pastry dough to a 12-inch round and transfer to the baking sheet. Mound fruit in center of the crust and fold a 2-inch edge all around the fruit filling. Brush edges of pastry crust with heavy cream and sprinkle with coarse sugar. Bake crostata for 30 minutes or until the fruit is tender and the crust is a golden brown.

Note

Cool the crostata by placing the baking sheet on wire rack for 15 minutes. Cut into slices and serve.

Have a Seat

ACKNOWLEDGMENTS

We call every person who comes into Beekman 1802 a "neighbor"—no matter where in the world they happen to be. We are so grateful for the friendship, the support, and the inspiration from each of them. They helped us get a fourth cookbook into the world.

Every member of the Sharon Springs community and the surrounding artisan community has contributed to our lives in ways that they cannot know and that we cannot eloquently communicate. We wish there were enough pages in this book to introduce each and every one of them to each and every one of you.

Rose Marie—thank you for all of your old ways that have become our new ways.

Christian Watson—thank you for constantly showing us a different way to see the world through both your pictures and your words.

And lastly thank you to everyone at Houghton Mifflin who understood exactly the love story we were trying to tell with this book. Every step of the way they assured us that what we were doing was as important as it was beautiful. Having a good neighbor is second only to having a good cheerleader.

Brent Ridge and Josh Kilmer-Purcell

Brent and Josh are the founders of Beekman 1802, the lifestyle company that centers around their farm in Sharon Springs, NY, and focuses on seasonal living. They were the stars for two seasons of *The Fabulous Beekman Boys* (Planet Green, Cooking Channel) and have been featured on *The Martha Stewart Show*, *Rachael Ray*, *The Dr. Oz Show*, NPR, *ABC World News Tonight with David Muir*, the *New York Times*, the *Wall Street Journal*, *Vogue*, and *Vanity Fair*, among others. Together they are the authors of three previous cookooks (*The Beekman 1802 Heirloom Cookbook*, *The Beekman 1802 Heirloom Dessert Cookbook*, and *The Beekman 1802 Heirloom Vegetable Cookbook*) and publish *Beekman 1802 Almanac*, a quarterly magazine. Their Beekman 1802 products have been featured in stores such as Target, Bed, Bath & Beyond, and Bloomingdales, Learn more about their life on the farm at **beekman1802.com**.

Rose Marie Trapani

Born in Sicily and now a neighbor to Josh and Brent in Sharon Springs, New York, Rose Marie has been cooking all her life. Read more about Rose Marie on page 31

Christian Watson, Photographer

Known for his work in fields of "made by hand," Watson's work concentrates on bringing back the fading stories and talents of prior generations. Specializing in film photography, pen and pencil, and antique goods—it remains forever important to Watson and his team at 1924US that the work done is one with a story.

Hard work, dedication, and continuous learning—traits passed on from his grandparents—are ones Watson hopes to pass along through his work.

INDEX

Note: Page references in *italics* indicate photographs.

A

Almond(s)
Boozy Bundt Cake, *74, 75*–76
Brittle, *128,* 129
The Essential Biscotti, 188–89, *189*
Fig Cookies, 124–25, *125*
Paste Cookies, 180, *180*
Pesto Trapanese, 28–30
Amaretto Icing, *74, 75*–76
Anchovies
Rib Eye Steak Palermo Style, *114,* 115
Tomato, Olive, and Caper Sauce, 102
Appetizers
Asparagus Crostata, 134–35, *135*–37
Bacon-Wrapped Stuffed Dates, 85, *85*
Braised Artichokes, 152–53, *153*
Crostini with Artichoke and Pea Pestos, 138–39, *139*
Fried Peppers with Balsamic Drizzle, 195, *195*
Goat Cheese–Filled Cherry Poppers, 194
Many Mini Arancine, 82–84, *83*
Mozzarella with Tomatoes, Cucumbers, and Pesto, 192, *192*
Quick Pickled Vegetables, 196
Ricotta-Filled Figs Wrapped in Prosciutto, 14, *15*
Zucchini Blossom Squares, 86, *87*
Zucchini Blossoms with Savory Ricotta, 199
Apricot Chicken Pot Pie, 118–20, *119*
Artichoke(s)
Braised, 152–53, *153*
Olive Salad, *88,* 89
Pesto, 138–39
Artisan profiles
Farmer John, 50
Jasmine Crowe, 68
Kip, 202
Michael McCarthy, 105
Rabbit Goody, 183
Rose Marie Trapani, 31–32

Arugula
Chicken Breasts with Roasted Red Pepper, Gremolata, and Prosciutto, 232–33, *233*
and Egg, Fried Chicken Cutlets with, 58, *59*
Goat Cheese–Filled Cherry Poppers, 194
Asparagus Crostata, 134–35, *135*–37

B

Bacon
Bread, 96, *97*
-Wrapped Stuffed Dates, 85, *85*
Basil
Artichoke Pesto, 138–39
Mozzarella with Tomatoes, Cucumbers, and Pesto, 192, *192*
and Parsley Pesto, 193
Pesto Trapanese, 28–30
Scallops Caprese, 236, *237*
Yogurt–Sour Cream Herb Sauce, *52,* 53–54
Bean(s)
Chick Pea Soup, 93
Maria's Vegetable Minestrone, 144, *145*
and Sausage Soup, 94, *95*
Beef
Braciole with Sunday Tomato Sauce, 170–72, *171*
Chili Masala, 112–13, *113*
Crowded Meatballs, 116
Rib Eye Steak Palermo Style, *114,* 115
Stuffed Onions, 154–55, *155*
Beet Greens Sautéed with Garlic and Breadcrumbs, 38, *39*
Biscotti, The Essential, 188–89, *189*
Breadcrumbs, Seasoned, 99
Bread(s)
Bacon, 96, *97*
Caramelized Onion–Walnut Focaccia, 148, *149*
Doreen's Scones, *146,* 147
Garlic Knots, *26,* 27
No-Knead Italian, 22–24, *25*

Panettone Ricotta Bombe, 130, *131*

Soup, Nonna's, 142

Brittle, Almond, *128,* 129

Broccoli

Burnt, Soup, Beekman, 18, *19*

with Garlic, 41, *41*

Broccoli Rabe and Sausage, Orecchiette Pasta with, 164, *165*

Butter

Brown, –Sage Sauce, 160–63, *161*

Ramp, 150, *150*

C

Cakes

Bundt, Boozy, *74,* 75–76

Chocolate Mousse, Salvation, 72, *73*

Olive Oil, A Thousand Different, *186,* 187

Cheese

Asparagus Crostata, 134–35, *135–37*

Bacon-Wrapped Stuffed Dates, 85, *85*

Blue, Potato Slices, 101, *101*

Braised Artichokes, 152–53, *153*

Caramelized Onion–Walnut Focaccia, 148, *149*

Chicken on a Stick, *151,* 173–75

Cream, Cookies, Ms. Cesa's, 184, *185*

Field Greens, Fig, and Brie Salad, 141, *141*

Garlic Knots, *26,* 27

Goat, –Filled Cherry Poppers, 194

Homemade Ricotta, 156, *157*

Many Mini Arancine, 82–84, *83*

Mozzarella with Tomatoes, Cucumbers, and Pesto, 192, *192*

Panettone Ricotta Bombe, 130, *131*

Raviolo Filled with Egg Yolk, 160–63, *161*

Ricotta-Filled Figs Wrapped in Prosciutto, 14, *15*

Seasoned Breadcrumbs, 99

Squash Manicotti, 46–49, *47*

St. Joseph's Day Cream Puffs, 126–27, *127*

Sweet Ravioli with Ricotta and Honey, 70, *71*

Zucchini Blossom Squares, 86, *87*

Zucchini Blossoms with Savory Ricotta, 199

Chicken

Apricot Pot Pie, 118–20, *119*

Breasts with Roasted Red Pepper, Gremolata, and Prosciutto, 232–33, *233*

Cacciatore alla Fortunata, 230–31, *231*

Cutlets, Fried, with Egg and Arugula, 58, *59*

Drumsticks in Wine, *60,* 61

on a Stick, *151,* 173–75

Chili, Beef, Masala, 112–13, *113*

Chocolate

The Essential Biscotti, 188–89, *189*

Fig Cookies, 124–25, *125*

Mousse Cake, Salvation, 72, 73

St. Joseph's Day Cream Puffs, 126–27, *127*

Cocktail, My Whey, 157, *157*

Cookies

Almond Paste, 180, *180*

Cream Cheese, Ms. Cesa's, 184, *185*

The Essential Biscotti, 188–89, *189*

Fig, 124–25, *125*

Taralle, One Perfect Mouthful, 77–78, *78*

Crab Cakes with Homemade Tartar Sauce, *178,* 179

Cream Puffs, St. Joseph's Day, 126–27, *127*

Crostatas

Asparagus, 134–35, *135–37*

Plum and Peach, 244, *245*

Crostini with Artichoke and Pea Pestos, 138–39, *139*

Cucumber(s)

-Dill Salad, 235

Tomatoes, and Pesto, Mozzarella with, 192, *192*

D

Dates, Bacon-Wrapped Stuffed, 85, *85*

Desserts. *See also* Cakes; Cookies

Almond Brittle, *128,* 129

In-a-Minute Icebox Lemon Semifreddo, *242,* 243

Lemon Granita, 181, *181*

Little Bits of Honey (*Struffoli*), 240–41, *241*

Panettone Ricotta Bombe, 130, *131*

Peaches and Wine, 238, *239*

Plum and Peach Crostata, 244, *245*

St. Joseph's Day Cream Puffs, 126–27, *127*

Sweet Ravioli with Ricotta and Honey, 70, *71*

E

Egg(s)

and Arugula, Fried Chicken Cutlets with, 58, *59*

Beef Braciole with Sunday Tomato Sauce, 170–72, *171*

Nonna's Bread Soup, 142

Poached, in Tomato Sauce, 106, *106*

Potato Frittata, *220*, 221

Spaghetti Frittata, 159

Yolk, Raviolo Filled with, 160–63, *161*

Espresso, preparing, 76

F

Fennel

-Orange Salad, 200, *201*

and Sardines, Perciatelli (Hollow) Pasta with, 224–25, *225*

Spice Rub, 107

Fig(s)

Cookies, 124–25, *125*

Field Greens, and Brie Salad, 141, *141*

Ricotta-Filled, Wrapped in Prosciutto, 14, *15*

Fish. *See also* Anchovies

Baked Salmon with Tomato and Green Peppercorn Butter, 234

Pan-seared Swordfish with Ginger, Soy, and Chives, 176, *177*

Perciatelli (Hollow) Pasta with Fennel and Sardines, 224–25, *225*

Flour, Toasted, Soup, Megan's, 21

Focaccia, Caramelized Onion–Walnut, 148, *149*

Frittatas

Potato, *220*, 221

Spaghetti, 159

G

Garlic

and Breadcrumbs, Beet Greens Sautéed with, 38, *39*

Broccoli with, 41, *41*

Fennel Spice Rub, 107

Knots, *26*, 27

Lemon Sauce, 37

Seasoned Breadcrumbs, 99

Ginger, Soy, and Chives, Pan-seared Swordfish with, 176, *177*

Granita, Lemon, 181, *181*

Grape Leaves

Brined, 17

how to use, 16

Greens. *See also* Arugula

Beet, Sautéed with Garlic and Breadcrumbs, 38, *39*

Brined Grape Leaves, 17

Field, Fig, and Brie Salad, 141, *141*

H

Herb(s). *See also specific herbs*

Sauce, Yogurt–Sour Cream, *52*, 53–54

Honey, Little Bits of *(Struffoli),* 240–41, *241*

I

Icing

Amaretto, *74*, 75–76

Lemon, 77–78, *78*

L

Lemon(s)

Fennel Spice Rub, 107

Garlic Sauce, 37

Granita, 181, *181*

Icing, 77–78, *78*

Sauce, Linguine with, 222, *223*

Scallops Limoncello, *66*, 67

Semifreddo, In-a-Minute Icebox, *242*, 243

St. Joseph's Day Cream Puffs, 126–27, *127*

Lentil Soup, Christian's, 206, *207*

Limoncello

Panettone Ricotta Bombe, 130, *131*

Scallops, *66*, 67

Lobster

Crusted, with Oregano Butter, *62*, 63

Fruit of the Sea Salad, 90–92, *91*

M

Meatballs, Crowded, 116

Mint

Artichoke Pesto, 138–39

Pea Pesto, 139

Pesto Trapanese, 28–30

Mushroom(s)

with Cream, 100, *100*

Nonna's Bread Soup, 142

Risotto, *166*, 167

Veal Swiss Style, 109, *110–11*

Mussels
    with Breadcrumbs, 64, *65*
    The Devil's Stew, 122, *123*
    Fruit of the Sea Salad, 90–92, *91*
    with White Wine and Cream, 121, *121*

N

Nuts. *See* Almond(s); Pine nuts; Pistachios;
    Walnut(s)

O

Olive Oil Cakes, A Thousand Different, *186,* 187
Olive(s)
    Fruit of the Sea Salad, 90–92, *91*
    Homemade Tartar Sauce, *178,* 179
    Rose Marie's Pork Chops, 168, *169*
    Salad, *88,* 89
    Tomato, and Caper Sauce, 102
Onion(s)
    Caramelized, –Walnut Focaccia, 148, *149*
    Megan's Toasted Flour Soup, 21
    Stuffed, 154–55, *155*
Orange(s)
    -Fennel Salad, 200, *201*
    Fig Cookies, 124–25, *125*
    A Thousand Different Olive Oil Cakes, *186,* 187

P

Panettone Ricotta Bombe, 130, *131*
Parsley
    Artichoke Pesto, 138–39
    and Basil Pesto, 193
    Lemon Garlic Sauce, 37
    Mussels with Breadcrumbs, 64, *65*
    Pesto Trapanese, 28–30
    Seasoned Breadcrumbs, 99
Pasta
    alla Tavola, tradition of, 117
    The Devil's Stew, 122, *123*
    Homemade, 43–45, *45*
    Linguine with Lemon Sauce, 222, *223*
    Maria's Vegetable Minestrone, 144, *145*
    Orecchiette, with Sausage and Broccoli Rabe,
        164, *165*
    Perciatelli (Hollow), with Fennel and Sardines,
        224–25, *225*

Pesto Trapanese, 28–30
Raviolo Filled with Egg Yolk, 160–63, *161*
Sausage and Bean Soup, 94, *95*
Spaetzle, 108, *110–11*
Spaghetti Frittata, 159
Squash Manicotti, 46–49, *47*
Star Baby Soup, *204, 205*
Sweet Ravioli with Ricotta and Honey, 70, *71*
vegetable substitutes for, 216–17, *217*
Warm Orzo Salad, 229, *229*
Peach(es)
    and Plum Crostata, 244, *245*
    and Wine, 238, *239*
Pea(s)
    Baby, Sautéed, 151, *151*
    Pesto, 139
Pepper(s)
    Beef Chili Masala, 112–13, *113*
    Chicken Cacciatore alla Fortunata, 230–31,
        231
    Fried, with Balsamic Drizzle, 195, *195*
    Fruit of the Sea Salad, 90–92, *91*
    Goat Cheese–Filled Cherry Poppers, 194
    Grilled Summer Vegetables, 214, *215*
    Olive Salad, *88,* 89
    Roasted Red, Gremolata, and Prosciutto,
        Chicken Breasts with, 232–33, *233*
Pesto
    Artichoke, 138–39
    Basil and Parsley, 193
    Pea, 139
    Trapanese, 28–30
Pickled Vegetables, Quick, 196
Pies
    Pot, Chicken Apricot, 118–20, *119*
    Tomato, 212, *213*
Pine nuts
    Basil and Parsley Pesto, 193
    Beef Braciole with Sunday Tomato Sauce,
        170–72, *171*
    Linguine with Lemon Sauce, 222, *223*
    Pea Pesto, 139
Pistachios
    The Essential Biscotti, 188–89, *189*
    St. Joseph's Day Cream Puffs, 126–27, *127*
Pizza Dough, Breakfast of Champions, 208

Plum and Peach Crostata, 244, *245*
Pork. *See also* Bacon; Prosciutto; Sausage(s)
    Chops, Rose Marie's, 168, *169*
    Ribs, Brown-Sugared, with Bourbon BBQ
        Sauce, 226–27, *227*
    Tenderloin, Spiced, with Warm Orzo Salad,
        228–29, *229*
Potato(es)
    Beef Chili Masala, 112–13, *113*
    Frittata, *220*, 221
    and Sausages, Fire-Pit Grilled, 56
    Slices, Blue Cheese, 101, *101*
Pot Pie, Chicken Apricot, 118–20, *119*
Prosciutto
    Ricotta-Filled Figs Wrapped in, 14, *15*
    Roasted Red Pepper, and Gremolata, Chicken
        Breasts with, 232–33, *233*

R
Ramp Butter, 150, *150*
Ravioli, Sweet, with Ricotta and Honey, 70, *71*
Raviolo Filled with Egg Yolk, 160–63, *161*
Rice
    Many Mini Arancine, 82–84, *83*
    Mushroom Risotto, *166*, 167
Rosemary
    Fennel Spice Rub, 107
    A Thousand Different Olive Oil Cakes, *186*, 187

S
Sage
    –Brown Butter Sauce, 160–63, *161*
    Veal Swiss Style, 109, *110–11*
Salads
    Cucumber-Dill, 235
    Field Greens, Fig, and Brie, 141, *141*
    Fruit of the Sea, 90–92, *91*
    Olive, *88*, 89
    Orange-Fennel, 200, *201*
    Orzo, Warm, 229, *229*
Salami
    Beef Braciole with Sunday Tomato Sauce,
        170–72, *171*
    Chicken on a Stick, *151*, 173–75
    Rose Marie's Pork Chops, 168, *169*
    Zucchini Blossom Squares, 86, *87*

Salmon, Baked, with Tomato and Green
    Peppercorn Butter, 234
Sardines and Fennel, Perciatelli (Hollow) Pasta
    with, 224–25, *225*
Sauces. *See also* Pesto
    Béchamel, 46–48
    Lemon Garlic, 37
    Raw Tomato, 209, *209*
    Sage–Brown Butter, 160–63, *161*
    Tartar, Homemade, *178*, 179
    Tomato, Olive, and Caper, 102
    Tomato, Sunday, Beef Braciole with, 170–72, *171*
    Yogurt–Sour Cream Herb, *52*, 53–54
Sausage(s). *See also* Salami
    and Bean Soup, 94, *95*
    and Broccoli Rabe, Orecchiette Pasta with, 164,
        165
    and Potatoes, Fire-Pit Grilled, 56
    Stuffed Onions, 154–55, *155*
Scallops
    Caprese, 236, *237*
    The Devil's Stew, 122, *123*
    Fruit of the Sea Salad, 90–92, *91*
    Limoncello, *66*, 67
Scones, Doreen's, *146*, 147
Semifreddo, In-a-Minute Icebox Lemon, *242*, 243
Shellfish
    Crab Cakes with Homemade Tartar Sauce, *178*,
        179
    Crusted Lobster with Oregano Butter, *62*, 63
    The Devil's Stew, 122, *123*
    Fruit of the Sea Salad, 90–92, *91*
    Mussels with Breadcrumbs, 64, *65*
    Mussels with White Wine and Cream, 121, *121*
    Scallops Caprese, 236, *237*
    Scallops Limoncello, *66*, 67
Shrimp
    The Devil's Stew, 122, *123*
    Fruit of the Sea Salad, 90–92, *91*
Soups
    Bread, Nonna's, 142
    Burnt Broccoli, Beekman, 18, *19*
    Chick Pea, 93
    Lentil, Christian's, 206, *207*
    Maria's Vegetable Minestrone, 144, *145*
    Sausage and Bean, 94, *95*

Star Baby, *204, 205*
Toasted Flour, Megan's, 21
Sour Cream–Yogurt Herb Sauce, *52,* 53–54
Spaetzle, 108, *110–11*
Spice Rub, Fennel, 107
Squash. *See also* Zucchini
    Baked Spaghetti, "Noodles," 216–17, *217*
    Manicotti, 46–49, *47*
Stew, The Devil's, 122, *123*
Struffoli (Little Bits of Honey), 240–41, *241*
Swordfish, Pan-seared, with Ginger, Soy, and
    Chives, 176, *177*

T

Tomato(es)
    Beef Chili Masala, 112–13, *113*
    Chicken Apricot Pot Pie, 118–20, *119*
    Chicken Cacciatore alla Fortunata, 230–31, *231*
    Cucumbers, and Pesto, Mozzarella with, 192,
        192
    The Devil's Stew, 122, *123*
    and Green Peppercorn Butter, Baked Salmon
        with, 234
    Grilled Summer Vegetables, 214, *215*
    Nonna's Bread Soup, 142
    Olive, and Caper Sauce, 102
    Paste, Homemade, 34, *35*
    Pesto Trapanese, 28–30
    Pie, 212, *213*
    Sauce, Poached Eggs in, 106, *106*
    Sauce, Raw, 209, *209*
    Sauce, Sunday, Beef Braciole with, 170–72, *171*
    Scallops Caprese, 236, *237*
Turkey Club Roast, *52,* 53–54

V

Veal Swiss Style, 109, *110–11*
Vegetable(s). *See also specific vegetables*
    Minestrone, Maria's, 144, *145*
    Quick Pickled, 196
    Summer, Grilled, 214, *215*

W

Walnut(s)
    Artichoke Pesto, 138–39
    –Caramelized Onion Focaccia, 148, *149*

Fig Cookies, 124–25, *125*
Whey Cocktail, My, 157, *157*
Wine, Peaches and, 238, *239*

Y

Yogurt–Sour Cream Herb Sauce, *52,* 53–54

Z

Zucchini
    Blossom Squares, 86, *87*
    Blossoms with Savory Ricotta, 199
    Grilled Summer Vegetables, 214, *215*
    "Noodles," 216–17, *217*
    Sausage and Bean Soup, 94, *95*

BRENT RIDGE and **JOSH KILMER-PURCELL** are the founders of Beekman 1802, the lifestyle company centered around their farm in Sharon Springs, NY, and focused on seasonal living. They were the stars for two seasons of *The Fabulous Beekman Boys* (Planet Green, Cooking Channel) and have been featured on numerous television shows and in national magazines. Together they are the authors of three previous cookbooks and publish *Beekman 1802 Almanac*, a quarterly magazine. Their Beekman 1802 products are featured in major national retailers. Learn more about their life on the farm at beekman1802.com.